THE EASY TO FOLLOW LEADER

Your Simplified Guide to Thriving in Leadership

Kris Mailepors

The Easy to Follow Leader
Your Simplified Guide to Thriving in Leadership
By Kris Mailepors © 2018

Hardcover ISBN: 978-1-61206-165-8
Softcover ISBN: 978-1-61206-166-5
eBook ISBN: 978-1-61206-167-2

Cover & Interior Design: Fusion Creative Works, FusionCW.com
Lead Editor: Jennifer Regner

For more information, visit EasytoFollowLeader.com

To purchase this book at highly discounted prices, go to AlohaPublishing.com or email alohapublishing@gmail.com.

Published by

ALOHA
PUBLISHING

AlohaPublishing.com

Printed in the United States of America

This book is dedicated with a heavy heart to the voiceless . . .
May your barbaric YAWP be heard from the rooftops.

Contents

Values are how your seeds of greatness sprout. Human beings are much like plants—either growing or dying. There is no status quo.

—Kris Mailepors

Introduction

When you are easy to follow, people around you feel safe and supported. They will put in the effort to follow; they aren't afraid of screwing it up or wasting that effort. This means you are bringing a level of authenticity and clarity to your world from which others can benefit. Your spouse can love you better when they know clearly what you need and when it's important. Your kids tend to find what they are good at when they are given clear encouragement; what I learned from the Boys & Girls Clubs is that every kid needs an adult in their life who they don't want to disappoint. Most people never outgrow that need.

Being easy to follow is about opening up what is most naturally important to you or your business. It's about demonstrating those values with your behavior. It's about recognizing it in others, so it's reinforced. The result is a culture where people thrive and results soar.

How Can You Be an Easy-to-Follow Leader?

The best advice I ever got as a leader, years ago in one of my first leadership opportunities, is central to everything this book will discuss. It's a story about how being authentic is simultaneously the scariest, most difficult, and at the same time the easiest thing about being a successful leader.

In 1999, as a new sales manager in a new area, I was failing. My primary job was recruiting and training a sales team. I had been in the role for a full year, and by every metric imaginable, I was failing. In context, my peers around the country were experiencing great results and overall, the company's growth was soaring. The problem was me.

I have always thought of myself as a good student—willing to learn. So I asked successful managers and other leaders in the organization how I could improve. I got a lot of advice that, at the time, seemed relevant and important. I was 22 years old, young for the ranking manager in northern New England. I looked even younger than my age. I was given advice like, "Grow a beard to look older" (I still don't think I had the hormones to be successful at that), "You have some suits that are a little outdated, maybe update your wardrobe," and my favorite: "You're too nice, Kris. People will walk all over you. You should be tougher and less nice to people."

I heard some version of the "you're too nice, toughen up" from a lot of people, so I figured it was good advice (and a lot less expensive than a fleet of new suits). As it turns out, that advice was bad, and following it took my failures from bad to worse. As an independent contractor, I wasn't making salary. I was making only commissions from a failing office and still had to pay all the bills. At some point, this 22-year-old had to come to the realization that this job

I thought was a major career move for me was a door about to slam shut—leaving me broke, in debt, dejected, and rejected.

When I was close to giving up, I got what the company referred to as a "field visit." This was where one of the executives overseeing the region spent some quality time with a manager to wax philosophic about some big-picture thinking. A man who, even today, I still consider to be my mentor made this visit to observe me. What I got was the only good advice I received as a young and growing leader.

He observed me for no more than two minutes, as I carried out my solution to the "you're too nice" advice with some potential recruits. He pulled me aside and privately gave me advice for the ages:

"Kris, stop being a jerk. You're bad at it."

I was overcome with humility. He was right. I was trying to be more gruff, short, aloof, and generally trying to be tough. It felt to me like I was being "to the point," "strong," and projecting a "tell-it-like-it-is" attitude.

Does this sound familiar? I've met many leaders who habitually wear those behaviors proudly, like awards. In reality, it just makes people not want to work hard for them.

This mentor leveled that atomic mic-drop at me and in 30 seconds gave me an alternate script for a part of my interview where I thought I was "demonstrating my toughness." The new approach was nice ("nice" had become a cussword to me), but it had strength and confidence. It worked.

Starting that very evening, some of the metrics that were "failing" immediately became among the top five in the nation among 350-plus managers. That persisted for years to come—just like that. A mentor connected me to something that was authentic for me. I worked a few more successful years in that company, and I earned a reputation for being a strong and enthusiastic leader who was widely loved by his teams and peers.

I wanted to share this personal story of failure "gone good." For almost 20 years, I've kept this close to me when I see people taking the "wrong good advice." (Note: I don't think there's such a thing as bad advice. Lots of good intention goes into it. But there's lots of wrong good advice, or at least good advice taken at the wrong time or by the wrong person).

Have You Been Here Before?

I like how leadership books try to claim to be the one-stop shop to turn a curious mind into executive material. While I appreciate the work that goes into creating the instruction, skills development, and inspiration that goes into such a book, very few of them take into account just how personal this leadership journey is for the person on it.

When I am teaching a leadership skill set to a group, I usually start by asking the group to break into small, intimate groups of three to five people and do a short activity. I ask that they do two things:

a. Agree on a list of the top 10 qualities or abilities leaders need to be great

b. Rank that top 10 by importance, with one being the most important

I've never seen two lists that were the same. Why is that? Sure, words like listening, honesty, integrity, and communication almost always show up. But they always show up in different ranks of importance, and with different counterparts on the list.

That gets me thinking. That list is always dependent on some variables:

- Who in the small group is leading the discussion? They're not likely to be impartial (and no one asked them to be) and may be driving what's important in their mind.
- Each person is negotiating what they see as important to arrive at the end result. Some are eager to have their voice heard and some are more eager to arrive at the finished product, so they may facilitate completion of the list over pushing their favorites on the list.

The end result is always a lot of variation in the top-10 list for these groups.

The lesson? This notion of leadership is so deeply personal, it could never be one size fits all. What makes one person a great leader is individual to that person, and therefore what they see in other leaders is just as individual. A major milestone in one's professional growth is when they realize not everything they are told is perfect for *them*. Their strongest version of a leader is based on leadership strengths which may be different from those of that leader's leader, or of their peers.

Most people pick up their first book on leadership and are blown away by what they learned; it can become like gospel, their new way of life. However, for those who expose themselves to more resources, something happens: they start to see that some books ring *more true* than others. That's perfect! Individuals must use their critical eye when someone tells them what kind of leader to be. They should even use that eye when reading *this* book! Always be on the lookout for that good advice you shouldn't take. It's not all perfect for you.

Here's another lesson I got from doing this exercise that I only noticed in recent years. People don't list *skills* when they are asked for "qualities or things leaders need to be great." They list *values*. Quality, goal setting, project management, tech writing, or anything tangible like these almost never show up. Looking at terms like those, you could argue their place on such a list. The responses I get instead of "goal setting" are words like "visionary." Instead of "project management," I see "organized." People list *values*. That's how we see leadership. We define it and judge it in terms of values. Yet book after book and boss after boss will put a skill or skill set at the center of how to grow as a leader.

So there it is. That 1999 version of me, taking bad advice to heart, was being steered away from my values. Back then, I valued rapport with my team, trust, and supportiveness (I still do). Trying to be tougher and meaner did not ring true for me, and people just didn't trust what they saw. When I learned to be better about expressing how supportive I wanted to be, people came to me for that support in all its forms. There I was, a nice boss who could be as tough as he wanted because people knew that toughness was just support; I was actually encouraging them to raise their bar and persevere through challenge. They knew where my toughness was coming from. It wasn't about being tough for the sake of being tough; it was about having the grit to express my support no matter what, even if it was with toughness. For some people, I believed in them when they didn't, and that helped them. When I did that, I was carrying out my values *with toughness*, not making up a new value called toughness to create a leadership image.

I learned then that nothing is more important to a leader than values.

Nothing is more important to a leader than values.

Have values and stick to them. When your values are clear, things like project management, goal setting, conflict resolution, and motivating others will become effortless. That effortlessness will be explored throughout this work.

More importantly, have *your* values, not someone else's.

Let's say you are an Olympic swimmer. To be a complete athlete, you may take on many training methods to perform at the highest level. Your training includes swimming, but it may also include weight training, running, biking, and others. No matter what you add to your training regimen, swimming is where you are best, and it should always be your main focus. A marathon runner may try to tell you that you aren't a great distance runner and may want to make you a better distance runner. That may or may not have benefit for you. If you started listening to that marathoner as an "expert," it could take your focus away from what you're best at: swimming. That marathoner may have great advice, but it's just not ideal advice for a swimmer. And that marathoner may actually know nothing about swimming.

In real life, you may have a leader who has a low level of emotional expression; they carry themselves with a consistent, calm exterior. You may be a passionate person who isn't afraid to show emotion (I think you see where this is going). That leader may have difficulty identifying with your strength because he or she has different strengths, just as a marathoner may not be able to identify with a swimmer. That leader may go so far as to tell you your emotional expression is a weakness, that you shouldn't show emotion. Wrong—that is like the marathoner saying to the swimmer that they'll never win a marathon. All that is true, but the swimmer is in a different sport. They don't *need* to be a champion marathoner.

Is swimming better than running a marathon? Of course it isn't. Just like someone who shows emotion is not worse or better than someone who doesn't. A leader with strong emotions knows when to show emotion, and that leader also knows when not to. The goal should never be to stop doing what you naturally do best (i.e., to abandon your strengths and values). To do so is inauthentic.

We all have gifts that serve us and serve those who depend on us. That gifted Olympic swimmer, just like the person who has healthy emotions on display, will be better equipped to serve those who depend on them if they present their best gifts with regularity.

Your leaders—even the good ones—don't always have the best advice. Many leaders give guidance and advice that suits their own role as leaders. For instance, leaders who like public recognition usually default to appreciating others publicly. Leaders who have been best suited by tempering their approach, putting their heads down, and supporting a greater cause are likely to ask the same of others. Innovators may push their employees to innovate, even when it's risky.

Are your leaders creating more of themselves or are they trying to get the best version of you?

Introduction

You need to pay attention to whether their advice fits you—your skills, your desires, your values. And if their advice doesn't fit, thank them and move on. When you know your strengths and openly display them as central to your daily practice, you are authentic. Thus, without really trying, you are easier to follow. People see in you something that is relatable, something that is easy to understand.

People follow values. When people know who you are and what drives your decisions, they are more at ease when working with you. It's mystery and unpredictability that interfere with workplace trust.

So, first and foremost: look at advice with a critical eye. Protect yourself from the *wrong* good advice. Your leadership journey is yours and yours alone.

The only leadership advice you should ever follow should fit your own talents, your own heart, your own experiences. If someone tries to give you a key to success, don't forget to *cut the key* to fit your lock, not the other way around. Your greatness will be unlocked with the *right* good advice.

CHAPTER 1

Why Is It Important to Know Your Values?

It's not new that values are a big deal. Almost every company packages them with mission and vision statements. You may have worked in a place that posted them with high visibility where people eat lunch or with less visibility behind a copier.

Have you ever been in a culture where a leader quizzed random staff members on the company values? What does it mean to you if someone can rattle them off effortlessly—or if they have difficulty recalling them?

For organizations, values that make sense are the easiest to *live*, the easiest to work with. If a hospital puts *patient-centered care* or something like it as a value, no one forgets that one. They see it and live it every day. Buzzwords like *synergy* or *innovation* are harder for people to recall unless they're living it constantly.

It's not confusing to see a company like Apple list as their first value *to make great products* or for Amazon to list *customer obsession* as theirs. Those famous organizations are obvious and clear in how they operate. You expect that value because you see it, not because you went and looked it up.

So what about leaders? Whether you know it or not, people judge you less on your skills or abilities than you think. Your intelligence and expertise matter, but what matters more is how people *buy* you—or *buy in* to you. People are really buying your character, your values.

When you know someone who behaves unpredictably, it takes more mental effort to keep track of them. You naturally trust someone who is predictable; you know what to expect and that helps you see them as reliable. It works the same way with leaders.

Do people know what to expect from you? And is that expectation a positive one?

So step one is to ask yourself: Do you know your values? If you asked others around you to guess at *your* values, would the answers even align? For most people, it's not something you've thought much about; yet, clearly stated values make it easier for people to identify with you, to trust you, and to carry out actions to meet your needs. As a leader, your clear and visible values make you easier to follow.

. . . If people know you value honesty, and you make every effort to be honest and openly correct yourself if you've passed along misinformation (accidentally or intentionally), people will be honest with you and trust what you have to say as truth.

. . . If people know you value courage, and you make every effort to climb outside of your comfort zone and openly let others know when you're doing so, people will appreciate and respect your courage. They will be more likely to support your efforts with their own courage.

Why Is It Important to Know Your Values?

. . . If you value recognition, and you're open about other people knowing that it's important to you, people will see that effort when you recognize others. When you miss a chance to give recognition, they are more likely to cut you some slack because they know it's important to you. Others are more likely to come to you with opportunities for you to recognize the efforts of their peers.

See how this works? We can agree that there are plenty of benefits to having values and openly living them. But other than just showing up every day and trying to be a good person, you may have never bothered to be open and clear about your *values or why they are important to you.*

When you're clear about those values that *most* drive your actions, others immediately know how to act to support you. You effortlessly become easier to follow. And in doing this, you can become a better leader—with no need for an MBA or that special certificate from the local university, nor did you need to spend hours in a seminar learning how to say the perfect phrase to people in order to solve problem *X*. It was as simple as making more transparent what's most important to you. People sometimes self-correct when they know what is needed. We naturally want to succeed and please those who depend on us (kids, spouse, boss, a team, etc.).

If you don't know your values, how can anyone else? We're all just guessing here, trying to do our best, and in the process, no one is rowing the boat in the same direction. Values give people that direction. And they exist no matter where the leader is sitting that day.

People connect with your values.

People who depend on you *buy your values* ahead of any skill or knowledge you have.

When You Are an Easy-to-Follow Leader, What Will It Do for Your Career and Personal Life?

Clarity . . . you can see where you're going and how you can get there. That's what knowing your values and expressing them to your team can do.

When someone is easy to follow, it speaks to something profound. Most humans actually like to work hard at something worthwhile—that kind of effort gives meaning to their lives and creates feelings of engagement. When it's clear what we need to do and why we should care about it, most people will do it and do it very well. Being easy to follow is about tapping into that clarity.

Look at popular charities like Habitat for Humanity. It's hard work, but people know exactly what to do and why they are doing it; they call it a labor of love. I've supported local Boys and Girls Clubs, where I see overworked and underpaid staff on an absolute mission to give those kids a better future—and you'd be hard-pressed to find a more engaged team.

Leaders can drive thriving cultures when people don't see a complicated choreography—complicated messages or expectations can be intimidating. When they see familiar things and things that put them at ease, they can naturally relax and trust.

Difficult conversations become less difficult in an environment of trust. In such an environment, why you may be working harder on one project versus another is more openly discussed. People help each other when they know what is needed, and that need is clear and simple.

Why Is It Important to Know Your Values?

This speaks to approachability. At some point in your life, you may have known a leader who had an open-door policy, but no one ever used it. That's an example of a leader who wasn't approachable. They had the policy, but for some reason, people found it awkward, uncomfortable, unproductive, or more trouble than it was worth to walk through that door and talk about something challenging.

The true folly here was that leader may have thought everything was great because no one ever came to them to complain. But in reality, no one complained because there was no benefit in doing so; nothing positive ever got done. You may be able to relate to that, unfortunately, if you worked for such a boss, or knew someone who did. That is an example of a leader who isn't easy to follow.

Somehow, the approachable leader has set the stage that their door is open and if you bring a complaint to them, it will be heard and discussed in a manner that will satisfy you—even if it can't be resolved. Doesn't that sound simple? Easy? Unfortunately, every time a leader is defensive, evasive, or says, "You go figure it out," they undermine that good intention of having the open-door policy.

Being easy to follow comes from a lot of things. It's approachability. It's trust. It's authenticity. It's relatability. In our society, where cutting corners is sometimes admired, I don't want to sound trendy when I say being easy to follow is easy—but it is. It's actually effortless.

It's considerably harder to try to become some version of a great leader than it is to just *be* the leader you are. You can be that leader today. It takes less work than a comprehensive readout of your strengths and weaknesses. Growth and skills can always be added to your tool kit, but they don't make you a leader.

What Does It Look Like When They Won't Follow?

Let's be honest, sometimes anyone can be hard to follow. You're human and, in a high-pressure work situation, you may have expressed behaviors you wish you could take back. That's life.

First, come to terms with this: despite your best efforts, you occasionally screw up. You do things that make people sigh and shake their head when you leave the room. Welcome to leadership. Honestly, we've all worn the leadership hat that made us hard to follow.

So what does that look like?

Some leaders are introverts. They have to be careful that their natural need for solitude isn't seen as isolation. Someone who is seen as isolated is mysterious. How do we see mysterious people? Not with trust. We view them with caution and curiosity. That leader is being hard to follow.

Some leaders are intense. Really intense leaders have high energy—usually doing so much and learning and growing so quickly, that before they know it they are leading too far in front of the organization. They had every good intention to set the tone and a high bar of performance. We're afraid to bring to them things we need, because this leader appears to have no needs, so ours seem petty in their crazy world. I'm making tea, and they're boiling the ocean. An intense and high-performing leader can take an otherwise talented employee and render them insecure and timid without even trying to. That's hard to follow.

Some leaders are natural fixers. When someone comes to them with some difficulty, the leader springs into problem-solving mode. Sometimes that's a perfect response. Other times, people bring this to their leader not to have it fixed, but to have their support—to know that this struggle is not a failure. They may want to own it themselves, and they want their leader to have their back. Leaders who can't adapt appropriately are not approachable—again, hard to follow.

Some leaders are so eager to be liked and be impressive, they are lousy listeners. When they hear someone talking, they are so consumed with giving a lucid response, they miss half of what's being communicated. If a person is trying to share something with you and there is any indication that you aren't fully engaged in active listening, you're being hard to follow.

These examples illustrate that very common personalities and behaviors can make you inherently unapproachable. When you're even a little less than 100 percent approachable—even 99 percent approachable—you can assume that you're missing opportunities to lead effectively.

All leaders are under 100 percent, by the way. This means that sometimes people on your team won't bring you problems when they should, some stories you get are incomplete or sugar coated, and someone who's talented (after all, *you* hire only talented people, right?) isn't getting the motivation they need to succeed simply because there's a blind spot around what they need and what you're delivering (or vice versa).

Bad or hard-to-follow leaders do a lot of damage to a team and to a business. And the majority of this damage is unintentional and totally preventable—you're trying too hard. You need to simplify.

CHAPTER 2

Leadership Development Myths

Leadership development as it is done today utilizes many common practices that don't serve the leaders or the organizations applying them. Many of these practices are one size fits all and are used because they are easy and logical; they can be consistently applied. They spell out clear steps, but not always appropriate ones. Some methods, which people have believed in for years, have become stale, run their course, or in some cases were never useful in the first place. We'll call these *leadership development myths*.

Myth: Leadership Development Is a Problem to Be Solved

Our brains are thinking machines. Humans are natural problem-solvers and this tendency, when left unchecked, devours most positive leadership development efforts and turns them into black-and-white processes. It's *assembly-line leadership development*.

Assembly-line leadership development happens in a few ways; mostly it happens socially. Many organizations and CEOs approach leadership development as problem-solving, although no one calls it that. Their first step in leadership development is usually some gap analysis or other identification of weakness. These processes identify a problem or need in existing leadership and present it in data form so it's black and white; it's objective. Leadership development then becomes a series of goals and action plans to close these gaps and solve these identified problems.

Unless this approach is customized for each leader, it totally misses the point of leadership. And it's making bad leaders—generations of them. While great leaders can still emerge out of this type of system, it is often designed to ignore leaders' best strengths. Leadership teams who are chasing gaps (gaps that may or may not even have a business risk) end up missing opportunities to flourish and discover their true gifts.

The Problem With Simple Assessments

The first step in an assembly-line leadership development process is to define a leader's weaknesses or problems using assessments.

Leadership assessments don't usually take into account environments, temporary issues, or external circumstances.

Every few months, a leader may have new gaps to close. They (or their company) spend money on training to learn skills needed to close these gaps, then later reassess so new data can show those gaps were closed or reduced. Then they do it again. Wash, rinse, repeat. Sometimes an old gap resurfaces after a few years. Does that mean the leader lost the skill? This gets individuals caught up in a lot of tail chasing.

I have seen this practice in action and experienced it myself. It is a common and often ineffective method for leadership development. There are two reasons why:

First, environment and culture are central factors to effective leadership, and most leadership development efforts will ignore this. If a leader learns some skills and phrases to be better at "difficult conversations," (a common topic for a leadership development curriculum) they try to bring those back to their workplace. They are returning to an environment where the existing culture and behavior caused conversations to be difficult to begin with. Coming back to that same environment with a few new words to use is nice; it's some tools for your manager's toolbelt. However, the tools will not be effective in *that* environment.

We can be better served by not having the problem at all. Is more effort made in continually solving the problem when it comes up, or in creating a place where that problem isn't a problem? We'll return to that concept more in a later chapter.

Second, think of the last time you had a big training in your organization on a soft skill, something with a topic like "communication" or "change." People attended. They laughed and applauded for some dynamic speaker who was skilled at keeping your attention with dramatic pauses, humor, and simple how-tos. At the conclusion, attendees completed an evaluation in which they shared how great the program was and even wrote down what they'll do differently from then on. It's all well intended and would appear to be a success. But . . .

. . . Fast-forward three months. Ask each attendee to say how their business or performance is now better or improved because of that training. You'll get a lot of blank stares and vague answers like: "I really listen more now," or "I am better at helping people understand X." The answers could have been about almost any training they ever attended.

Sound familiar? Why didn't the training "stick"? The main reason is that training for the sake of training or solving an organizational problem doesn't address the culture and environment that *triggered* the problem. Organizations spend money to train leaders, but one day later, leaders return to their environment and usually return to their existing habits.

The Problem With Company-Wide Training Events for All Leaders

Smaller and medium-sized organizations fall into the trap of trying to capture everyone (all managers and leaders) in a training event. They may have a "change management" seminar and make it mandatory to attend. A year later, there may be a new change and a fresh need to get some managers more resources on this topic. Decision-makers won't consider doing that training again because they already did it. Managers who could benefit from it may get labeled as low performers because they were previously trained in "change management" but are struggling with leading a team through a new change.

The "we already did that" response to training is a real problem. It doesn't address anything relevant about the people or the organization. It takes a sexy topic and makes the *event* the center of leadership development, not the *people*. So many things about the business and its people can be different from one year to the next, even month to month. The C-suite of an organization like this is under the delusion that a training done a year ago somehow means the content is hardwired and actively being applied today. This assumption is just not true in most cases.

The other problem can be when new managers are hired into the organization any time after that big change management training. The organization simply doesn't bother addressing that the new managers don't have this knowledge. "We already did that," so it won't be offered again.

Leadership is a personal quest. The tools and training that stir you and motivate you will be different from those that motivate your boss, mentor, or other role model. Just like that activity where leaders get into groups and generate a list of 10 important leadership characteristics, there is variation. Billions of dollars are spent each year on leadership development. Are you starting to see that so much of it is not a "fit," or is outdated, or just not relevantly applied for the person experiencing it?

More Leadership Myths

There are other false assumptions actively driving leadership development in organizations all over the world. Here is a short list:

Myth: Experience Is the Best Teacher

It's true, we learn from our experiences. That problem-solver brain takes past experiences and imposes them on the people around you today. Be careful not to generalize too much or assume the next person will behave the same way as the last person did.

If you've filled an important position and your last experience with a person in that role was difficult in some way, your view of their work will likely be seen through that lens. You could be making many assumptions and limiting the new person without even knowing it.

Your experiences are a reference point, but when it comes to how a leader interacts with her/his team, past experiences are largely irrelevant. Every person and circumstance is unique—unless you perpetuate a situation through your expectations.

This plays out in how we treat our family, too. If you are used to being criticized by a parent, everything they say may be heard through that filter and could easily trigger you. We are responsible for how that relationship is *today* because we play a role in sustaining how we approach it *today*. Our experiences shape our behavior, and this isn't always positive. If you view a person (a coworker, your sibling, etc.) as difficult, you shape your approach to them because you're expecting them to be difficult today; don't be surprised if difficulty is what you get. As a reference, your experiences should be tempered and adjusted to view your landscape with the most relevant lens possible.

Your best teachers are people and circumstances that you see in this exact moment; they should guide you. Your experiences should *not*. I was once told I couldn't succeed in a territory where others had a consistent track record of failing. I saw some of that failure firsthand, but when I viewed the opportunity with a new lens, my result was a number one sales ranking among 150 new managers in the Eastern U.S. for that year.

Myth: Leaders Are Born. No, Leaders Are Made. No, It's Both. Wait, It's Neither.

Much has been discussed in other books on whether leaders are born or made. I won't beat that drum here, but I will give you an analogy that makes it clear to me. Think of leadership as if it was a sport you know, like baseball. Pretty much anybody can pick up a bat and ball and play baseball with someone. They can learn the rules. They can practice to their heart's content. Some people will dedicate their lives to it. Some people are gifted at baseball and don't need to practice very much and could even be major league all-stars. Others practice endlessly and may never see their dreams fulfilled. Most people who practice and put in a lot of effort can be successful at it.

This is true for leadership, or any other endeavor. Some people are naturally gifted to excel, if given the right environment. And anyone can be successful if they apply themselves. Yes, anyone. There is a leader in all of us, and the right situations will bring it out.

Myth: Leadership Is Charisma

Only really charismatic and politically adept people can lead? This is just untrue—it is a folly that can set a leader up for failure. A naturally introverted leader may pick up a book on charisma written by and for extroverts. That leader reads the book and innocently tries to assume the identity of "charisma." The problem is that it doesn't quite fit. Charisma is a set of behaviors; some of those might benefit some leaders, some might benefit others, and some leaders will benefit from none of it. A good leader may have charisma; some of their behaviors may naturally display this. Charisma is not required to be a strong leader.

Myth: The Boss Must Be the Leader

It may be true that the boss sets the rules. However, there are lots of instances where this isn't the case. Many teams in the start-up world operate more like a sports team than a hierarchy. There is a coach, and the coach is the closest thing to a boss. Yes, the coach makes the rules and must be a good leader, but often there is a team captain who is really the one leading the team. That's the person others depend on for advice and as the role model for behavior.

Myth: Leaders Are Impeccable (Superhero Illusion)

It's true, we hold leaders to a higher standard than we do our peers. The real truth is leaders are human and fallible. They are imperfect. They might be just as scared and awkward about **giving** feedback as you are about **receiving** it, for example.

When leaders allow themselves to be seen as normal—as perfectly flawed—they've immediately become more approachable and relatable. It's natural that they are held to a higher standard of behavior and performance than their teams, but why? No one has a really good answer to that. I believe in role modeling behavior, but not at the expense of being human, authentic, or if it makes a leader somehow separate from and unrelatable to a team. Because of this, many leaders put effort into hiding their flaws, their humanness.

Myth: The Leader Knows Best

Just like experience isn't always the best teacher and leaders aren't impeccable characters, leaders don't always know best. An old Japanese proverb says, "No one in the room is as smart as everyone in the room." Not even the leader. Often the most challenging issues can most easily be solved by the people who are closest to it. That expertise can exist in anyone.

Myth: Leadership Is Defined by Authority

Sometimes defined as "positional" leadership, this is also wrong. The real authority comes from teams, not leaders. If you don't believe that, walk into our nation's largest department store chain and shout "Strike." You'll get some attention. Leaders have the ability to use authority, but when overused or used improperly, people don't put up with it.

It's more accurate to say leadership is *influence*. Anyone can have influence, even if they have no official authority. I've held positions and professional relationships where I had no direct reports. That technically meant I had no authority. What I had was influence. Influence is usually developed over time. Influence is a currency, and it's earned with credibility. When people trust you and see you as useful, you have credibility. That credibility gives you influence. Authority alone does not. I've heard some political scientists say that in a democracy, the highest office in the land isn't the U.S. President, it's the office of *citizen*. Public officials are elected to serve the public. Even the U.S. President works for us, not the other way around. Although we don't usually "elect" our workplace leaders, in many ways we hold their success in our hands. If we don't follow, they're not leading.

Myth: To Improve Your Leadership, You Must Learn More Skills

It's counterintuitive, but as a leader embarks on learning and skills development, they can become a worse leader. That's right. This happens to most of us, and only some of us are lucky enough to catch it. For instance, if a leader learns a language of "difficult conversations" at a conference or from a training or book, but no one around them has that same vocabulary, they might have no way of connecting to others in a meaningful way. The leader's attempts to demonstrate their keen new ability can even be more divisive and adversarial than what they were doing previously. Difficult conversations just got more difficult.

Many leaders advance so quickly and are leading so far out in front, they lose their team in the rear-view mirror. I've seen VPs and chief officers spend a lot of time and effort building external allies and collaborations with existing or potential competitors in their communities and industries. This kind of effort is critical, especially in a twenty-first century economy. The great business mind Michael E. Porter calls this *coopetition*, and some leaders excel at it. This may be great for business, but gradually, the teams they are leaving behind start to feel neglected. This is not a minor or irrelevant problem.

The same thing can happen in families. Sometimes parents are working their butts off trying to make ends meet. The kids just want Dad home to read to them or play with them. Dad might call them ungrateful; after all, he's putting a roof over their heads and food on the table. But everyone knows the main thing kids need is time. As adults, we're not much different. Much of the effort leaders put in for the business is undermining their ability to lead (and be followed by) the people actually running the business.

Myth: Leadership Training Is Just for Leaders

Solo learning, or learning in a vacuum, can distance a leader from their team. Yet most leadership development activities are given to the leader alone, not with their team. And we wonder why leaders and teams sometimes don't connect.

Another major force acting against a leader is the gap between what teams are giving for effort presently and what they could be giving. One role of a leader is to get the most from their teams. This is achieved through four cultural aspects of the work environment:

1. Expectations of work and outputs are clear.

2. Team members have sufficient purpose or reason to pursue expectations (the famous "what's in it for them"). Also called the *why*.

3. Resources needed to pursue expectations are accessible.

4. Team members are supported so they can navigate the barriers to completing the expectations, or the barriers are removed altogether.

These four aspects of the workplace are central to a leader's success. If any one of these four aren't maximized, leadership is missing the point. Leaders can beat any other drum to get their team to perform, but it will fall on deaf ears if these other things are missing.

Leaders can get lots of skills from books or conferences, but the reality is that, to achieve the results they need, they are largely chasing smaller problems caused by one or more of these four things going wrong.

Myth: Leadership Training Aimed at the Symptoms Is Effective

Most of the tail-chasing leadership development that goes on today is ineffective because it's misguided. It's chasing a symptom of a problem, not the problem. If someone tears their ACL in their knee, they feel pain. The problem is a torn ligament, and the pain is a symptom.

I want to be clear: we may see the pain as a problem, but it's not the main problem. You want to fix the knee. If you only address the pain and not the knee, you may have bigger and more persistent problems later. Organizations spend a lot of effort responding to symptoms as if they were problems and not solving the real problems. Let's review an example of this:

You go to HR because you need some team building: you are seeing people being short with each other, not communicating workflows, and talking behind each other's back. You perceive poor teamwork, so you address it by engaging in team building. This is addressing the pain, not the knee. Doing a round of trust falls or the game "two truths and a lie" won't change any of the symptoms described above. The only benefit will probably come from the team agreeing that it was a waste of time and laughing about it when the manager isn't in the room.

So what fixes the problem that is causing this symptom? It's probably not trust falls. It's finding out where the breeches of trust are and addressing them, not forcing people to trust people they don't otherwise want to trust. Approaches that are naturally resisted simply aren't sustainable, even if a boss makes it mandatory. People aren't distrustful of coworkers because they don't know how to trust; it's because they are protecting or guarding something important to them, like part of their work. Question the communication flows around work handoffs. Discuss why it's okay to talk about others who aren't in the room when it shouldn't be. These efforts do more to address the problem, rather than address the symptom of the problem.

A leader who may need to improve how they handle tough conversations shouldn't learn "difficult conversations"—they should learn about what is making important conversations difficult. They may learn that they are not supportive, or they are not open to input or suggestions. They may learn they just avoid difficult situations because they are conflict averse. Forcing them to engage in those difficult conversations with special phrases won't go well. It's like being forced to dance before you are willing to do so voluntarily. It doesn't feel right, and it looks much worse. They could learn to be more approachable overall, to be clearer with values and expectations so fewer difficult situations arise.

What's *Not* a Myth

Leadership matters.

That may be an obvious statement. What many don't realize is that when it's done improperly, it can do a lot of damage to the morale and engagement of a team, and organizations spend a lot of money for it. Living under the assumptions that these myths can support or sustain leadership is a very real challenge—and threat— to the success of your business and career. The rest of this book is about unlocking the natural and instinctive leader within you.

CHAPTER 3

Why Leadership Matters

Better Leaders Get Better Results

Leaders are the face of the corporate stage. They are behind the effort when a team is motivated to a level they may not otherwise reach. They are needed to get results and to have the courage to change and improve already functional organizations.

Good leaders are a company's most valuable asset, not only in combined salaries but in the costs associated with leader attrition. Leaders are the most important and sought-after competitive advantage a company can have. Head hunting is a $200-billion-dollar industry in the twenty-first century. Leader turnover can affect stock prices, employee engagement, and intellectual property—and those are the good ones.

The bad leaders—and these aren't necessarily bad people—can do a lot of damage to the morale of your team while you are trying to deliver your mission to your customers. It's no surprise that the attributes of successful leadership have been debated, discussed, and published widely.

What Do Leaders *Do*?

Many people have said that leaders and managers just get in the way of good work. That's true in many ways. Bad leaders can do a lot of damage, and micromanagers can slow and stifle good work with their misdirected attempts to improve it. Great leaders get great results. Better leaders get better results. This is the simplest way to define a leader's success. In whatever way you define your benchmarks, a good leader should be able to improve them in a sustainable way.

It's that simple. If "no leader" means that a team's results, however you define them, can be better, then "no leader" is a possible option. Often, having no leader can be better than a bad leader. Sometimes, a bad leader leaves a situation and there is an immediate boost to morale, productivity, engagement, or any other metric. That boost may not be sustainable, but it's proof that leadership matters. Even if you don't agree that leaders are needed, we can all agree that we can do without poor leadership.

With jobs getting more complex and bosses trying to squeeze more into the workday, getting sustained workforce performance is more difficult and more critical than it's ever been. Hard-working people need leadership to sustain performance.

Leaders provide the framework where good performance becomes great. They guide and support people when a bad situation could be otherwise unbearable. There is a good leader in all of us, but there's also a mistake-prone, bad leader in all of us. All leaders stray; I have strayed and so have you. The very best ones know how to be accountable to those who depend on them.

Leaders Create Trust

A 2016 study from Wellesley and the University of Kansas illustrated that we (humans) are hardwired to trust people who are similar to us. In a workplace, there is normally a lot of diversity. If it's a healthy organization, there is diversity of opinion and personality, too. Let that sink in. That means we're hardwired as human beings to not easily trust our workplace environment. That is why people are sometimes slow to adapt to requests for change. They don't trust a change when they already trust the things that are known to them. It's also why people under-communicate at work. It's why so many teams and individuals aren't engaged or living up to their potential.

Trust. This is the foundation on which we build leadership. Let me illustrate why this is critical in leadership.

Leadership is relational. Every interaction is boosted, hindered, or blocked altogether, based on the trust that exists there. Where trust is high, sometimes just a look across the room can start a cascade of positive activity. Where trust is inconsistent, more time and effort must be put into getting that same activity cascade, to set the expectations and directions.

Where trust is broken, commitments must be solidified and more following-up may be required. If you think that sounds like a lot of effort, you're correct. Leaders spend a lot of time doing this work, and it feels like they are busy to the point of burnout. All that work is tail chasing and unnecessary, but those leaders would never admit that. All that work could be minimized if a trusting environment was properly cultivated.

Often a leader doesn't even have the time to build foundations of trust, as it may interfere with day-to-day needs of the business; their own leader or VP may be stifling this. This is a no-win situation.

Trust is foundational to everything leadership. Now bear this in mind: *everyone* thinks they can be trusted. If you ask 100 people if they are trustworthy, 100 will respond favorably (even if some qualify their "yes" a little). Yet most people say they know or work with people who are not totally trustworthy.

Think about that perception gap; there are people who don't trust you in spite of your best efforts to be trustworthy. When you act or communicate, you are trying to come across a certain way to align with your intent. When you're perceived, sometimes that's out of alignment with your intent. This communication model shows what I mean:

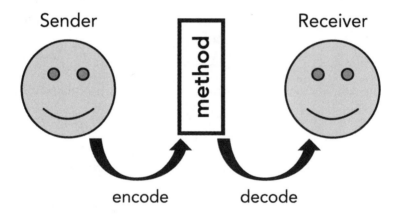

This demonstrates the gap between what you intend to communicate, how you convey it (encode), and how your actions or words are received (decoded) by others.

Like throwing a football, the passer is responsible for throwing a pass that's easy to catch. Even then, it's dropped sometimes. Passers must take care that the ball is where the receiver can see it, without the sun in their eyes, so they don't have to stretch or change their own direction. Ideally, the receiver should need to do as little adjustment as possible to "receive" the message.

Why Leadership Matters

Charles Feltman wrote *The Thin Book of Trust: An Essential Primer for Building Trust at Work* (Thin Book Publishing, 2008). I like this book because he takes something that seems very vague and subjective—trust—and boils it down to four simple competencies: sincerity, reliability, competence, and care. If you are paying attention to those in your interactions, you'll actively build trust. I want to touch on these, specific to leadership.

Sincerity, in my interpretation, is how a leader can demonstrate authenticity and clarity. In the football analogy, this is the effort the quarterback puts into making a throw easy to catch. Authenticity is that general sense of what you say is what people can believe. Compliments are genuine. If you say something, you act like you mean it. One can be sincere, but if they are also forgetful or disorganized, there's a common workplace challenge with the next trust competency: reliability.

Reliability is how closely a leader honors her or his commitments. When you look at your calendar, you probably can identify one or two upcoming meetings where you give the other person about a 50/50 chance of moving or canceling the meeting. Sometimes you double book that slot because of that likelihood. That person may be sincere, but they are not reliable. I have many conversations with VPs and C-suite executives about reliability. Their schedules are in high demand. But when they continuously bump and postpone time with the people who need them, they are incidentally creating a poor reputation. They are also communicating an attitude about whose time is important. As a great leader, be on the better side of honoring most of your commitments. Be someone others can count on. They'll trust you more when you *say* you'll do something.

The Easy to Follow Leader

Competence is the most straightforward, yet the most complicated for a leader. Most organizational structures are built for a leader overseeing a team of experts. Naturally, experts and frontline employees have more expertise than their leader. Leaders should openly acknowledge this, yet most pretend they know more than they actually do. To be fair, experts shouldn't expect their leader to know more than (or even as much as) the expert does, but they should expect their leader to know enough to support a productive workplace culture. These were listed in the previous chapter but here they are again to remind us of how a leader can demonstrate competence when expertise may be unnecessary:

1. Expectations of work and outputs are clear.
2. Team members have sufficient purpose or reason to pursue expectations (the famous "what's in it for them?"). This is also called the *why*.
3. Resources needed to pursue expectations are accessible.
4. Team members are supported so they can navigate the barriers to completing the expectations, or the barriers are removed altogether.

Care is the most obvious, and it is also the most neglected. One hundred percent of the leaders I speak to tell me, "Of course I care about my team!" They can get quite defensive when asked such a question, yet so many people want more from their leaders when it comes to this. When I ask leaders, "Can you tell me something you did this week (for a person or group) explicitly to make sure they know you care?" I get a lot of blank stares. Most leaders realize here that they can *do* more to connect with the people they appreciate.

Trust—it's like a house of cards. It takes time and patience to build. One bad move or slip, and the whole house comes down;

years of effort can literally collapse with a single breath. The whole house falls, not just part of it. It can be rebuilt, but it can require the same amount of time and effort just to get back to where you were. This is why the effort to build and sustain trust is so important to leadership relationships. Most of the time, neither side recognizes the effort needed to rebuild trust, so poor relationships persist.

To be the leader who is easy to follow, people must be able to trust you with minimal effort on their part. That requires the leader to have this as a focus. Know how your behavior builds or blows down your house of cards. Know not just how you are trying to be, know how you come across.

Temet nosce
(Know thyself).

To see yourself as others see you is a most salutary gift.

—Aldous Huxley

More on the Superhero Illusion

Most of what is written in this book makes the assumption that you are reading it from the point of view of the leader. Take a moment to put yourself in the shoes of someone who is being led and consider a leader you have or once had, someone you either liked or disliked. How were your expectations of this leader different from the expectations you had for peers or yourself? Have you wondered why it's different?

There is a part of everyone that sees our leaders as infallible and holds them to a higher standard. Think of hearing a coworker chatting with another; you overhear them gossiping about someone. You may be against gossip, but the gossip itself may be relatively benign, such as someone leaving printouts on the printer and how they're annoyed when they do it. Now imagine if that same gossip is happening, and your boss is the one gossiping; or if your boss is the one violating the printer etiquette. It's somehow different, isn't it? We get a little extra agitated when it's the boss violating some of the environment's unwritten rules.

Why is that? Why are we more likely to turn to someone to vent about the boss's behavior when it's out of line? We have this attitude that makes us say, "They should know better." You may huff quietly when a coworker shows up late and a little disheveled, but when the boss does it, it's a big dent in the respect you may have for her or him, and you may remember it longer.

We automatically hold authority figures in higher esteem and to higher standards, and we view them with a little extra scrutiny and even skepticism. That's because they are, indeed, the authority. The fact is, when it comes to the sloppy habits and broken workplace rules, the boss *should* behave better.

It's like parenting. When we're kids, we think our parents are infallible—like superheroes. If your dad told you something when you were six years old, you could openly broadcast it as truth to anyone you knew at school. "Of course it's true, my dad said it," you could say. Yet as an adult, you'd sound ridiculous citing your father as the authority for any point you're trying to make at work.

Why Leadership Matters

Now that you're an adult, have you seen other parents interact with their own small children at the grocery store? You may
hear a child ask the same kind of curiosity questions that you did
when you were little. Then, in response, you may hear the parent say
something that is completely false because they know which answers
will prompt more questions and which ones will end the question
thread. That parent may just be innocently and whimsically saying
to their kid: "The sky is blue because, because, um, that's the color
of space and God likes blue the best."

That answer may have no basis in reality, but to that kid, the
answer is now a categorical fact. Kids see their parents as perfect
beings . . . which may be why as teenagers, when we start to understand human folly, we wrestle with our parent's hypocritical behaviors and suddenly there is a gap between who they are and who
we need them to be (or who we always thought they were). This is
at the heart of why a leader's relationships are complex and why,
when most people leave a job, they are leaving their boss more than
anything, according to a now-famous 2015 Gallup survey.

*I believe a major turning point everyone has in their relationships
with their parents is, as they reach their twenties and thirties, they
start to see parents as fallible human beings. They remember about
themselves that they weren't easy to deal with as kids. They begin
to see their parents had problems and flaws they never recognized
because their parents were trying so hard to be good stewards of their
children's growth.*

*This fallibility is human nature, and our relationships with our
parents improve when we understand this about them. We, in
effect, lift these superhero personas and stop holding them to heroic*

standards. When we see them as people, those flaws don't irk us as much. Granting our leaders this same humanity makes it a lot easier to follow them.

Back to leadership. We don't usually think of our leaders being just as flawed as we may be. When they go home at night, they overcook the pasta, lose battles with their teenagers or spouse, leave wet towels on the floor, maybe pay the electric bill late, even accidentally snap at someone's incorrect dishwasher loading. Translate those natural human tendencies to the workplace. They may be lost when it comes to navigating someone's dominant personality that is causing workplace difficulty among peers. They may hide their flaws fiercely because they fear losing the tenuous respect they have from their team. They may give you advice that is genuinely thoughtful but is just wrong for your situation.

They are human. When you understand this, you can cut them slack. When you start to cut your leader some slack, these missteps won't bother you as much, if at all. Missteps won't interfere with your ability to trust and lean on your leader as a true role model in other ways. Their work (or parts of it) may be great, even if their personality hasn't grown as fast as their career.

The reciprocal act here is leaders expressing their humanity when they can. This is important. If a leader is trying to show everyone how perfect they can be, their imperfections will stifle that image and stand out as blights. If a leader just lets their humanness show, openly and honestly, in a way that isn't destructive to others, their wholeness can be more accepted, and these imperfections will not be a hindrance.

Leaders who openly discuss what may not be working, not as a fault but as a simple issue, will set the tone for all conversations like that to be easy. "Difficult conversations" just got less difficult, and you didn't even need to go to a conference for an expensive workbook to add to your collection.

To be a supportive part of your team's culture, the best thing any of us can do is realize that in spite of someone's role as manager, VP of *X*, or a C-suite position, that human being has the same challenges in family and character as the rest of us. Did their flaw really ruin your life? Even if it's making extra work or anguish for you, find out how you can be more supportive of your leader. Don't just dig in your heels with high expectations.

And if you're a leader, allow me to convince you here that no matter how "relatable" you think you are, people are applying this impossible standard to you, and you're carrying it out for them. It's okay to ask for the same slack you're now willing to give your own leaders. Tell people you're human. Openly talk about your flaws, so people can know them and help you grow through them; those are the obstacles people face when navigating your road map. Help them work with you as a leader. It'll surprise you how much this authenticity, humility, and relatability will strengthen your support.

Why Is Leadership Hard?

Very few people have an appreciation for the responsibility that comes with being a leader. As we grow a career, we must grow, too. In many conversations with leaders, I have discussed some of the more subjective, hazy, and downright baffling things about leading a team of diverse and complex human beings. At some point, I end up telling them: "Welcome to leadership. This is why it pays more. It's harder."

The Easy to Follow Leader

Put to rest any delusion you may have that life as a leader is somehow easier because you get to tell people to do things for you. I'll make the case later that leadership is actually an effortless endeavor—but only when you're mindful of your surroundings and the most open version of you. Getting there can be tough.

Along the way, leaders are given many people-related challenges that will tax their logic.

The Black-and-White Manager

I've engaged some of my best coaching relationships with managers who attest that they are very black and white; and that philosophy serves them well. They tell me that they are the same with everyone, and consistency is important. The black-and-white manager inevitably encounters challenging situations—we'll call them grey areas—that don't cleanly fit their black-and-white philosophies.

Often, these managers like to look at every situation through this lens so it fits, and they can act or respond accordingly. That manager may have a late-night shift to fill that nobody wants. The simple and logical solution is to distribute that shift evenly, to force everyone to share a little bit of the burden equally. Go team. That never takes into account that people's reasons for not wanting that shift might vary. It could be a late Friday afternoon shift. Person A avoids it because they like to unwind Friday at the dog park. Person B avoids it because she takes Friday afternoon to travel out of state to spend the weekend with a terminally sick family member. Equity is black and white, but clearly there's an opportunity to view this scenario with some discretion and realize those reasons are not equal or parallel in their importance to the people involved.

Fairness and equality are simply different things. A black-and-white manager sees creating equality as the way to be impeccably fair to the team. Here's a critical point: leadership exists in the grey areas . . . even if "management" can be largely black and white. That's where a leader earns her/his stripes: navigating the grey areas where black-and-white rules simply don't work well. Managers and leaders who brag about being "black and white," like it's some badge of transparency, miss this opportunity completely.

About being totally black and white—it's not transparent, it's rigid. If you were really operating in a completely black-and-white system of decisions, a primate or an algorithm could do your job. That's a fact. Leadership isn't that simple. It requires judgment, subjectivity, and interpretation of situations as they arise. Individuals within a team all have different needs. Leaders must be calculating and thoughtful about exercising judgment, or they could be seen as having favorites. Navigating the waters of the grey areas successfully in ways that build trust and the right culture is an easy-to-follow leader's measure of success.

Always remember: fairness and equality are not the same thing.

Leaders Model the Way

Another important reason why leadership matters is this: leaders model the way. Gandhi famously said, "Be the change you want to see in the world." In a lot of ways, people imitate their models, for better or worse.

No matter how hard we try not to, we become our parents in some ways. That can be positive and negative at the same time. There is deep hardwiring at play there, and you could argue that this is genetic and/or learned. Well, in the same ways, teams are often a reflection of their boss.

Recently, I was with a team of peers and we were discussing how our teams were truly a reflection of us. Managers who were high energy had teams who were high energy. Contrastingly, managers who were struggling or had a lousy attitude seemed to be asking for help with a team who was also acting like this. In short, our takeaway that day was, "Your team is a reflection of you. If you're awesome, they are awesome. If your team sucks, it's because you suck." There is truth to that, and it speaks to why leaders matter. They model the way.

Let me share a story about a manager with whom I worked as a peer for about four years. The fictional name I gave her is "Last-Minute Monica." She was easily one of the most talented leaders I ever met. She had such an energy and zeal for her people; she put their success above everything. It showed, as her people performed at some of the highest levels in the country. Her amazing talents were enough to overcome a pretty severe lack of organization. This disorganization was obvious, as she was consistently 30-45 minutes late to our weekly staff meetings and was rarely prepared for them.

It is true, Boston traffic was never easy, but others planned for that to arrive on time. At these meetings, her metrics reporting was poor and rushed (usually calling back to her office for an assistant to dig through the data). We used metrics and statistics as measures of who was doing which part of the business well, and we'd discuss how we can improve. These numbers were obviously being guesstimated and she was winging it to report them. These reports resembled cocktail napkins with scratches on them more than a formal business report.

Here's the thing: Monica didn't need to do reports to be successful; her overall output was breaking sales records. She completed her
reports because the whole division was asked to. Here's the simple
lesson in the Last-Minute Monica story: she openly admitted that
she didn't pay much attention to some of the administrative tasks in
her world and that she was disorganized.

Monica had such enormous talent that she could get by without
taking time to do these reports. The problem, however, was never
with Monica, it was with people who developed into leaders under
her. They didn't have her level of talent yet followed her lead (it was
the only "way" they saw modeled). To Monica, it was enough to say
to them, "Do as I say, not as I do." She openly preached that this
was how she set standards around things at which she herself was
terrible, saying "I don't ever do these reports, but you should." She
was telling leadership candidates how to do parts of the business she
clearly didn't make any time for, herself.

> *"Do as I say, not as I do." Imagine an alcoholic parent telling their
> teenage kid to not drink and using the same phrase. The kid can
> hear it, see behavior that deviates from the directive, and know
> immediately that they can get away with drinking. After all, if it
> was really that important, the parent would follow their own rules
> better. People have finely tuned "B.S. meters" to identify these exact
> hypocrisies. The workplace isn't any different.*

It should come as no shock that new managers who developed
under Last-Minute Monica over the years had similar track records
when it came to their own organizational skills and reporting. Most
of them didn't have Monica's talent to make up for it, so the lack
of organization and reporting limited their success. Many failed as
new managers. Without good reporting, it was hard to pinpoint

gaps and help them effectively improve the business. Other leaders who were on top of such reporting could see where they were losing money or productivity. Some of Monica's managers succeeded, but they did so with big organizational deficiencies. However, they also learned some of the great habits and skills of their talented leader.

The lesson here is that leaders must *be* the change they want to see in the world. A leader can hardly ask their team to be transparent if they themselves are not. A leader cannot expect teams to openly discuss feedback if the leader doesn't model it openly and correctly. If a leader's desk is a disaster area, they cannot be taken seriously to ask anyone on their team to keep a tidy workspace. The phrase "Do as I say, not as I do" must be abjectly eliminated from your arsenal of leadership tools.

If a leader is courageous, they can ask it of their people. If a leader is organized and detail oriented, they are better positioned to ask it of their people. If a leader treats her or his people with respect, she or he can ask it of the team in return.

I learned this when I looked around my desk and saw a disaster area. I took a cue from other leaders with messy work areas who said things like "I have a system; it hasn't failed me yet." That may be true but think about my ability to sit down with anyone and ask them to be more organized. I'd look like a hypocrite. If I wanted *others* to be organized, I knew I'd have to model it some way.

Leadership matters because leaders model the way. Sometimes that's the manager, sometimes that's an informal leader on the team. Leadership is hard when we make it hard. Modeling the way isn't hard. While it may have taken some effort to clean my desk, it made asking others to be organized a heck of a lot easier and authentic.

Leaders Set the Tone

As leaders learn how important it is to model the way, a shift happens. If you could ask the sky if it's hard to be big enough for the birds to fly, the sky may tell you it is not hard or easy, it just "is."

Leadership: be the sky in which others may soar.

You are a great leader already, today. Leaders try on a lot of skills, in trying to be a better "sky." When a lot of effort is exerted doing this, it is usually wasted. Imagine a murky puddle. To see through it, you might try to stir it, sweeping the dirt away. In reality, that just makes it cloudier. Stop, let it settle, and the puddle becomes clear. The effort of putting in less effort—this creates a clear benefit in this example.

The best leadership is as natural and easy as letting that puddle settle.

To be your best leader, trying really hard to "do" things, learn skills, and be the general manager of all things, might just be muddying your waters. People may be in the boat, they might be paddling furiously, but they may be doing so out of sync, out of unison. Clarity exists in the cloudy puddle already. It simply emerges. When that happens, everyone can see. The great leader is already in you; it's not at the end of some long, mysterious journey. It's effortless.

Creating the sky in which others can soar isn't creation at all. It's there naturally. It's opening your mind to the idea that with less effort than you are giving today, you can be the leader you are made to be. You can be easy to follow—easier to follow than you are today. You are naturally authentic; we all are. That's the whole point of authenticity. The act of trying to be authentic isn't authentic at all.

Trying to be authentic isn't authentic at all.

Still with me?

The leader who is easy to follow is still working hard, still highly functional at the business. They are just not trying so hard to be all things. The leader who is easy to follow is a catalyst. Intelligent, skilled people will achieve things on their own, but when that leader is aware of the four main needs of the workplace, people on their team achieve more easily. These four needs are listed again below:

1. Expectations of work and outputs are clear.
2. Team members have sufficient purpose or reason to pursue expectations (the famous "What's in it for them?"). This is also called the *why*.
3. There is an environment where resources to pursue expectations are accessible.
4. Team members are given support to navigate the barriers to completing the expectations, or the barriers are removed altogether.

The same effort goes farther, like the group in a boat paddling. More paddling is irrelevant to success if it's not in sync. To the person paddling, they only know their own effort, and it's maxed out. When in sync, less effort is needed to achieve results. The same workday is less consumed with burnout and challenge. A leader can be the one who catalyzes this approach.

"Tough Love" Is Toughest on the Leader

One of my favorite interactions with a leader is working with them on the concept of tough love. It is one of the most difficult areas of leadership to fully understand and do well. Most of you have seen or experienced this in many forms. The most typical form is the one that doesn't work very well.

Here's what you may have seen because it's common. Bad tough love is when a manager digs in her/his heels and braces for a difficult conversation. They say something that may cause the other person to deny it or become defensive. The manager then punctuates their point by saying, "I'm giving you tough love." In other words, some people use the phrase "tough love" as a license to be unfiltered, tactless, and say things in the easiest (and sometimes the least positive) way—because the listener is supposed to just take tough love like a kick in the gut and grow from it.

Well, like an actual kick in the gut, it doesn't really help. It hurts a lot and doesn't really make you stronger. If anything, you only learn to protect yourself from future kicks. That doesn't always mean building up a stronger core and more broad awareness. It just may mean not opening up to that manager as much, so getting kicked is less likely, or just shielding them from certain information. That happens. Improperly applied tough love may be ruining your culture.

Let's do a little thought experiment. Think back to a time when you got some tough love that actually worked. Someone gave you some sort of input that was tough for you to hear. They did it in a way that meant something to you—you listened. You probably understood that something important was at stake. I bet as you recall that conversation today, you see it as valuable; you're grateful. That conversation may have involved tough love.

So think about this: If tough love is done right, on whom is it toughest? That's right, the person *giving* it. If tough love is done so the listener understands the message, why it's being delivered and what to do about it, that delivery is *much* harder on the person delivering the message.

I once worked with a healthcare manager who found a way to use a great phrase when she was delivering tough feedback to help one of her employees. She'd say, "This might be difficult for you to hear, because it's also difficult for me to say." What I love about that delivery is she is relating to the role she is playing in the difficulty, sharing ownership of the issue and not pointing a finger. Immediately when she says this, part of the listener wants to be compassionate to her rather than adversarial. It was a pretty effective way for her to deliver difficult information or feedback.

Giving people tough love should be tougher on you than it should be on the person receiving it. How do you do that? In the past, did you just get right to the point like a straight shooter? If you did, it was probably met with denial or resistance of some sort. I know that because I've seen it a million times. Bodies of work like *Fierce Conversations: Achieving Success at Work and in Life One Conversation at a Time* (Berkeley, 2004) by Susan Scott, and *Nonviolent Communication: A Language of Life* (Puddledancer Press, 2015) by Marshall Rosenberg have fantastic models to package and deliver conversations like I am suggesting. Rather than weigh you down with scripting, I find their advice to be clear and authentic.

It's less about being direct, mean, or tough. They may give scripting, wording, and phrases, but the spirit of their work is shining your authenticity, clarity, vulnerability, and trust.

Tough love comes from a place of authenticity. The good news is that tough love is made of the character you already have within you. It causes the greatest and most positive changes in others. It should always be toughest on the leader who delivers it, not the person who receives it. If done right, people should remember fondly when tough love was given to them.

CHAPTER 4

Why Values Matter

Your values are the simplest way to facilitate your work relationships. Communicating and demonstrating them helps people see you, observe your behavior, and relate to you—positively or negatively.

This is a big factor: how people connect to their leaders is how they relate to them. Trust is the foundation of this. Nothing productive can happen in a work relationship until trust is a functional, working piece of that relationship.

Theodore Roosevelt is credited with saying, "Nobody cares how much you know, until they know how much you care." In leadership tenets, this again brings us back to trust as a foundation. However, there is a deeper meaning for leaders in this quote. It tells us that, as a leader, your skills or intelligence are largely irrelevant with respect to your values and with respect to how you make your people feel about your relationship with these values.

Why Do People Follow Values Over Skills?

Let's be clear. People may admire you for your knowledge or skills. They may respect you. But for them to be truly motivated, they have to trust you, they have to relate to you, and they have to align with you. None of this exactly means they must like you, but it doesn't hurt.

Your relationships are your best assets as a leader. Your skills and your intelligence are important, but they don't do much for these relationships. Once you've made trust an important piece of your relationships, your values are the key to unlock everything a leader needs to be successful.

Your values are the key to unlock everything a leader needs to be successful.

Your values are what people see. People don't necessarily see your knowledge, but they may see you repeatedly touting it, and what they are really seeing is a value or character trait—arrogance. That knowledge suddenly gets a little less impressive. Your values can be what guides and drives people when you're not in the room, and this works both positively and negatively. It's the wake you leave behind after your interactions.

Following Skills Doesn't Work

Laurence Peter coined the term "Peter Principle." This is when leaders are promoted based on a high level of skill or performance at one level; once they leave the position where they are using those skills, their promotion takes them to the level of their incompetence. This means that good and skilled people bring their skills to a leadership role, but in the new role, those skills may be irrelevant. It's where talented *people* fail as *leaders*. There isn't any completely accurate data on this, but many articles assert that about 50-60% of new managers fail in their first year. Those odds are slightly worse than a coin flip. When it comes to a company's most valuable asset, that track record is downright poor.

Why do organizations make that mistake? Why do they assume the best welder makes the best foreman? Why do they assume the best nurse makes the best nurse manager? Time and time again, organizations lean on this method of leader recruitment. Whether or not it ends well is a crapshoot for most organizations. You've seen it—a leader who may be an expert in the industry but seems to have no command of the department, the team, the processes, or its functions. It doesn't work, and a lot of damage can be done along the way. That failed manager didn't just show up like the person who crashes a party and ends up ruining it. That was a long, drawn-out, calculated decision to hire or promote them; the decision and ensuing process to dismiss someone—or manage them out of the company—can be even more drawn out.

Organizations make this mistake because selecting such a leader is a clear, data-driven, black-and-white decision. A hiring manager might say, "Look, this person is a high performer, she/he has earned a promotion to the next level." This hiring manager is trying to live in a black-and-white world when, in reality, we're surrounded by the many shades and subtleties of grey. Anticipating how someone will do in a new environment with new metrics, a new job description, and new people around them takes a lot more than a few hypothetical interview questions.

How Do You Identify and Recruit a Leader?

So what piece is missing? Values. If this recruiting process was focused on values, recruiters could put their finger on what values they want to see (it could be a list of six or so from hundreds of possibilities). Would a candidate for that role align with, support, and drive those values? This focus is not on skills, although skills such as communication may be necessary to recognize the values you want to see.

Is *safety* a value for a workplace of a maintenance team? Yes. Would that leader who was promoted from a skilled maintenance team member make safety a priority? They would if they demonstrated that value before they were promoted. How would they demonstrate it? How would they recognize it in others? How would they spot breaches of safety and coach others in these instances? We could be more certain they would continue to do those things as a leader if they did these things as a team member. Choose the values you want to see in your leaders.

Put simply, when a new leader emerges on the scene, values are the first thing people will sniff out. The theme of ABC's hit show Designated Survivor demonstrates how this can work. It is about a lower-level cabinet member (Kiefer Sutherland) who is suddenly appointed President of the United States after a terrorist attack wipes out most of the ranking federal government. He is a soft-spoken, bookish man who was HUD secretary before being thrust into a role with demands that were over his head. The character is doubted, undermined, and certainly not trusted to fill the needs of the role.

He makes his values more important than any political advice he receives. He's warned that this is a poor strategy, but it gradually builds support and alliances. Words like sincerity, authenticity, and integrity are used frequently to describe him. In a short time, he builds the trust of most of the people around him. He's predictable in his behavior, so people also trust that. Any perception of weakness is quickly overcome by his strong belief in what's right.

All of this new leader's tough decisions are driven by his values, even when the odds are stacked against that decision benefiting his agenda. Immediately, this character is likable as a new leader and as a family man. His values make him heroic in building alliances and achieving against the odds. In many modern political climates, a predictable, authentic, sincere, values-driven leader might seem like science fiction, but this is a person to whom other characters and viewers alike can relate.

In the workplace, in the family, and in any context, a leader's values are the things to which (or from which) people will most easily connect. The reverse is also true, as values can be what prompts people to disconnect from a leader. For instance, if a leader is insincere, people will immediately view his or her tactics with skepticism, even when the tactics are the proper ones.

Values can be compassion, courage, integrity, respect, or anything that is important to the work, the mission, or just to the people who show up every day. My leader might be very different from me in age, gender, religious or political beliefs, taste in food, taste in music, etc. If that leader has my trust and they value things that I also value, I am more likely to devote effort to support that leader. That's an easy to follow leader.

If I value *honesty,* and that leader has shown me that honesty is important to her/him, my trust in this person just got easier. I'll want to demonstrate honesty to her/him. That will show up in my work, how I share problems with that leader, and other ways. Most importantly, that leader is now extra accountable to be honest; any breach of honesty that is not addressed is a breach of trust in general.

You Don't Have to Be Perfect

If a leader who had identified honesty as a value is dishonest in some way (and we're all human, it doesn't necessarily make that leader a bad person) and they rectify it openly, they've actually maintained their connection to that value. Having a value and communicating it doesn't mean you can never make a mistake that violates that value.

Imagine a boat using navigation tools. You're the boat. The course is your behavior. The tools are your values—they guide you. You want to adhere to that course, but sometimes you stray; sometimes it's a little stray, sometimes it's a veer.

You may value *courage,* but on one day you totally chicken out of having a difficult conversation. Your values are what hold you accountable and prompt you to eventually express courage and have that conversation.

You can still be a strong and credible leader, even if you occasionally stray from your values. Many people are afraid to openly express their values because they recognize they haven't adhered to them perfectly. They fear they could look bad. Mark Twain was the likely source of the quote, "It's better to remain silent and be thought a fool than to open your mouth and remove all doubt." But, counterintuitively, people will find you more relatable when they see you have a value and wrestle imperfectly to adhere to it. People who see their leader that way will be more willing to do that themselves.

Consistency Is Key

If people perceive poor or inconsistent values in their leader, they are likely to carry out their own navigation. Here's what this can look like on a team: lots of people may be busy, but not unified. In the boat, this means everyone is paddling, but maybe just splashing in different directions. Everyone feels busy and productive in their bubble, but overall business functions may be struggling. Leaders try to increase process efficiency or hire more staff in these circumstances, and none of those solutions work. They tend to just amplify issues (more staff means more paddling out of sync) and outcomes aren't usually positive.

If you really think about it, you will realize people don't follow leaders. They follow that leader's values. They emulate and imitate values. They carry out work with those values as their own navigation tools. Their leader may be the vessel of those values; they are the model. Kouzes and Posner describe "modeling the way" and "clarifying values" as very early steps in their widely used leadership textbook *The Leadership Challenge: How to Make Extraordinary Things Happen in Organizations* (Jossey-Bass, 2012). It's their starting point on leadership structure for good reason.

Following a Value

When teams can perceive strong and consistent values, their own compass is in part guided by these cultural cues. For instance, if a leader holds *courage* as an important value in the context of work, it can mean that "we value courage in all interactions; we speak candidly, and openly give and accept feedback even when it's hard." If that's a value that guides people, giving feedback is no longer about the training one person receives to improve giving feedback. Everyone's using the same compass. When a tough conversation happens, everyone recognizes that it's hard, and therefore imperfect. Team members can cut each other slack when it comes to these conversations and recognize the courage it takes to have them. People are less defensive, less anxious, and therefore more open to the conversation.

In a team with this value, giving feedback effectively isn't a ***skill*** at all: it's a ***behavior*** rooted in the value of courage. The leader sets that tone and does her or his best to carry it out—freely admitting when that opportunity is missed. That leader will recognize others when they show courage and can encourage others who may be anxious or otherwise reluctant to have that conversation. Courage is the value that everyone understands, not a manual titled *How to Give Feedback*. When people know feedback is coming from a place of courage, and the courage is to carry out the mission as opposed to some personal conflict, the skill of giving feedback is irrelevant.

This is the power of values. People follow them because of the benefit. When a leader can be that model, teams operate far more effectively and the need for team-building training, communication training, and other solutions to perceived dysfunction melts away.

Do you really think humans need to be trained on how to talk? You might think *yes* because of the existing corporate culture and the billions of dollars that are spent on such training. Professionals can communicate just fine; the common ground of shared values (using the same compass and navigation tools) we all use as a guide is the easiest way to simplify any communication issue. It's the breaching of values and trust in the workplace that causes the problems associated with teams and leaders.

In a values-based workplace, team-building activities aren't needed to *fix* anything. Team-building activities can be done because they are fun; people can freely embrace the experience rather than dread it. Having the clear values *is* the skill of feedback, communication, conflict resolution, change management, and all the rest. Sure, there are tactics to executing change management, but in a workplace devoid of values, people will still paddle chaotically. In a values-driven workplace, the tactics associated with something like "change management training" are more about the paddling that is already aligned, and speeding it up, slowing it down, or changing its direction—while all are pulling in the same direction.

Values guide people in most aspects of their lives, consciously and unconsciously. Leaders model them, recognize them, and coach or support the people trying to stick to them.

How Values *Are* Team Culture

Organizational culture is based on values—good or bad—and those values will shape processes, expectations, follow-through, and accountability. When those values are destructive, dysfunction follows.

A lot has been written about changing an organizational culture. Looking at the landscape of all that literature, the underlying theme that emerges is *values drive culture*. Peter Drucker famously said, "Culture eats strategy for breakfast." This means that a well-planned initiative usually doesn't consider the actual human beings who must carry it out. People have a psychological resistance to change that varies in duration and reason from person to person. That's what devours an otherwise brilliantly thought out, perfectly logical plan.

At the heart of a team's culture are the values of that culture. What gets devoured in the strategy are the things that stray from the values as they presently exist. If a team holds *transparency* as a value, and an initiative is suddenly initiated with reasons that aren't clear but they are told to do this simply because it's important, the team will covertly or overtly resist and reject that initiative. This can look like foot-dragging, rumor-mongering, or generally questioning the change openly. Some leaders will label this natural resistance as individual low performance, poor attitude, or a lack of motivation.

If a workplace value is transparency, any initiative should be fully explained before it's rolled out—the team should have received some communication about ongoing involvement in (or explanation of) the change. This can be hard to do if there are confidentiality issues, yet these are the very breaches of value where trust is eroded. These situations can foster skepticism toward the decision-makers, and phrases like, "This is the flavor of the month" or "They have no idea what we actually do every day" describe what is said about the culture. These are the things that distance people from leaders and make leaders hard to follow—very hard.

The Myth of the Low Performer

I didn't include this myth in my list of leadership myths in an earlier chapter because it's pivotal to the theme of this chapter and may be a new perspective to anyone who has heard the term "low performer" before. Most behavior that may be perceived as unproductive, destructive, or dysfunctional stems from this type of failure to uphold values. It can also come from someone being pulled away from their values.

Understand that sometimes a person is simply not a fit for a role; sometimes a role evolves, and a person can change with it or seek something that fits better. That is their prerogative. But sometimes, low performance results because the demonstrated values in a workplace are demotivating; sometimes it's because no clear values are defined, leaving workers unsure about what is important or why work is being done in a particular way.

Throughout my career, I have been very critical of what I call lazy leadership (the term "lazy leader" does *not* imply anything about overall work ethic and talent. It refers to the level of effort and acumen toward self-awareness and understanding the needs of individuals around them). The idea that something called a "low performer" exists is, to me, a construct of lazy leadership. While I can understand sometimes there is a bad employee-role fit, there is no such thing as a low performer. A low performer is either unskilled to do the job (so train them), or isn't motivated to perform the job, and that's the responsibility of the leader. I hear many leaders say, "Some people just aren't motivated, no matter what." That leader has failed to find what motivates that person, and it's as simple as that. This is a place where leaders must be more accountable.

First, if a leader goes around eliminating low performers with regularity, they think that gets people to perform at a high level. There are data and articles to support that, too. But think for a minute what sort of culture that builds—what sort of values are guiding people. "High performance" isn't a value, by the way. High performance is a result of your values, i.e., a symptom of strong values. The sort of culture where, if someone is outside of the norm (they display poor attitude, behavior, or low performance), it can result in their dismissal from the company. This "cause and effect" only builds fear in others. As a consequence, this usually creates a culture where people don't speak up or want to stand out in any way; innovation is stifled and so is diversity.

Second, it's not as if low performers just showed up one day and started working. At some point, that person was recruited and vetted. Good judgment was used to bring them into the organization. They had some track record of experience, and if they didn't, they demonstrated some level of attitude or acumen to earn a spot on this team. References were checked. What goes wrong is the alignment with values and therefore motivation. The "unmotivated" employee is really just the alienated one.

It's the one whose work isn't connected to anything personally or professionally important. Human beings are amazing—all of them. They all have something that will light a positive fire in them and push them to excel. If you dismiss someone as unmotivated, you have failed to learn enough about this person to know what motivates them. You have also dismissed this human, further alienating them. That is lazy leadership.

The *low performer* is a myth, unless it's a term to reflect a lazy leader. Earlier, this book asserted that the team is a reflection of the leader. A leader who was not motivated enough to tap into a person's passions, when such passions were difficult to find, didn't motivate that person; that person is therefore not motivated. See how that works? Low or no motivation is a result of leadership failure. Even when it's due to a poor fit with the role, it's still the leader's job to manage that appropriately. This quote from Alexander den Heijer describes this well: "When a flower doesn't bloom, you fix the environment in which it grows, not the flower." Don't use the term "low performer" when you should really be using the term "low performance." This is an important distinction. Everyone is capable of high performance, and anyone can be capable of low performance. Try not to assign the label to people by using the word "performer."

Equally, the high performers on every team *have* discovered that passion—or had help from their leaders to discover it. They are motivated because their work is carrying out their values. Their effort and values (what's important to them) are in alignment. They see how having and following values can mean better teamwork, better fulfillment with their daily work, and more intention to follow the leader (and the leader's values).

Culture is key. Values are the rules of the culture.

Workplace culture, even a dysfunctional one, can be powerful. People adhere to the rules of the culture, sometimes with blind faith.

In a science experiment, five monkeys were placed in a room with a ladder with bananas on top. Every time a monkey went up the ladder, the scientists soaked the other monkeys with cold water.

After a while, every time a monkey would start up the ladder, the others would resist by pulling down the climber and beating him up. After a time, no monkey would dare try climbing the ladder, in spite of the banana reward waiting at the top.

The scientists then decided to replace one of the monkeys and cease the cold water treatment. The first thing this new monkey did was start to climb the ladder. Immediately, the others pulled him down and beat him up. After several attempts, the new monkey learned to never to go up the ladder. The behavior of the others was the only reason for the new monkey not to—it never saw the cold shower treatment.

The second monkey was substituted and the same occurred. The first monkey participated in the beating of the second monkey. A third monkey was changed and the same was repeated. The fourth monkey was changed, resulting in the same, then the fifth was finally replaced.

What was left was a group of five monkeys that never received a cold shower. And all five continued to prevent any new monkey from attempting to climb the ladder.

If it was possible to ask the monkeys why they beat up on all those who attempted to climb the ladder, their most likely answer would be, "It's just how things are done around here."

Does this story sound at all familiar?

This fable was inspired by the experiments of G.R. Stephenson, "Cultural Acquisition of a Specific Learned Response Among Rhesus Monkeys," Starek, D., Schneider, R., and Kuhn, H. J. (eds.), *Progress in Primatology*, Stuttgart: Fischer, pp. 279-288 (1967).

Workplace cultures are based entirely on the unwritten or written rules that come from the values of the leaders—and sometimes from employees. Things like respect, safety, innovation, courage, honesty, etc., can be part of these rules.

If that list of values is buried on some company website and doesn't exist anywhere meaningful, they do no good. To make your values *valuable* (excuse the homonym), they must be more than words—they must be *actions*. They must live in your culture and in the hearts, minds, and behaviors of the people. They must be self-evident.

Think of your organization. Do people know the organization's values? If they hesitate or can't name them, I ask you: *Why have them?* You have likely wasted a lot of graphic design getting them up on print media and/or the website.

Identifying Corporate Values

Most lists of corporate values are pieced together by first taking a group of senior leaders and asking, "What do we stand for?" (or something like that). If they're smart, they will seek input from staff and the front lines through some survey. From that question, there's a vetting process where some words are married like "results driven" and "initiative." Then, someone in power usually says, "Don't forget *X*," and a word like "innovation" gets added.

Does any of that sound familiar? That's a common way to do it. There are hundreds of ways you can do something very similar. It's not a bad process; it's a perfectly adequate way to land on the list. What is missing is the connection. Is it more connected to where your team is now, or where you want it to be?

This connection, this comparison to the current status is critical. If leadership thinks there is a cultural issue and people aren't as respectful as they should be, guess what may show up as a value? Respect. In principle I don't take issue with that method, or whether it was done covertly or overtly. The problem is when it sets up an expectation that those values are a "place we should get to." This approach psychologically distances people from that place, almost placing that gap in front of them. It's no wonder people aren't paying attention to corporate values enough to be living them daily.

Having values may be important, but are they the right ones? Do they mean something to a team as it exists today? Are they actually part of their daily work, or does effort need to be made to integrate them? A hospital can have *patient-centered care* as a value, and with every step and every part of every job, people can say and think, "We're here for the patient," and that simple mantra can endlessly motivate people. That same person can be deflated if the *respect* value is on a poster and they keep thinking, "We're supposed to be a culture of respect, but so-and-so doesn't act that way." That can be the total opposite of motivating.

I've pressed clients by asking them to name their organization's values. Almost no organization has a workforce in which everyone can name them effortlessly. If they can, it's sometimes because they were told to memorize them, but some of the words used like "synergy" may not mean anything to their day-to-day activity.

If they have them in their heart, and they'll tell you what they are before you can even ask, *that's* living your values.

Organizational Values Exercise

I encourage every organization of more than 10 people and all the way up to multinational organizations to do this values exercise:

1. **As a leader or member of a team, you can go through the list of core values (see appendix) and complete the simple statement "I value _____." where any word fills in that blank.**

   You'll know right away which ones fit your organization's needs more than others. As you find the six or fewer (don't exceed eight, that's too many for people to actually follow or remember) that truly resonate with you, your leadership peers, and/or your team, go to the next step:

2. **Complete this statement and the following two related statements for each value: "To demonstrate this value, I will _____."**

   You can have several answers to each value. This is one of your navigation tools. It gives you a set of commonsense behaviors that you'd probably do anyway. Completing this exercise is a small commitment to do these behaviors more transparently and intentionally. People should see you doing these behaviors and know (because you told them) that the behavior is because of the importance of the value (this is how leaders model the way).

3. **Complete this statement: "If I breach this value in any way, I will _____."**

   This is a reminder to you and others that it may be excusable to betray this value as long as, like any navigation tool, you recognize you are off course and adjust your course to follow it.

4. Finally, complete this statement: "When I see others demonstrating (value) by doing (behaviors), we should_____."

This will give you a set of cultural norms around how you encourage, serve, support, and most importantly, perpetuate that value.

The values themselves can be created through collaboration. Or, in some circumstances, it's appropriate for a leader to just create them and then share them with the team. The point is to have them. There may be some irony and hypocrisy in a leader stating, "I have unilaterally decided that *collaboration* is one of our team values." So exercise good judgment in how you arrive at your list.

This list of values can simply help you create and maintain personal relationships with stronger connections. Parents in a household where values are clear and followed (parents modeling the way) tend to raise kids who know and follow those values. Again, people follow a value more than they follow a person. Even the teenager who is engaging in reckless behavior is usually following some other value they aren't getting with consistency from home. A so-called bad influence may be a trusted friend, and that teen may not have an equally trusted place to go at home.

Values Build Trust

This exercise is common sense. It's so no-brainer, you may even be resisting the need to do it. But if some consultant like me came to your organization and started asking individuals what their values are (personal or organizational), would their answers indicate alignment? Would some answers be "I value honesty, unlike some people around here," or something similar to that?

Do this exercise. The trust you need, the alignment (read: buy-in) you need, the success you seek is critically dependent on it.

The culture you have—it comes from you, the leader. You can model the way. If you are trusted and you have clear values that you openly follow, you will build a culture where people can thrive. When you make mistakes and stray (and you *will* make mistakes and stray), you can openly acknowledge the mistake and what you did to correct it. If you recognize and support people who embody them, you will reinforce those values and people will follow those values everywhere they go; they will follow your model. They will follow your lead.

Values Build Culture

This method of developing your leadership abilities may be very distant from conventional leadership training as it currently exists in your world. This philosophy renders conventional leadership training mostly irrelevant. Most training you receive is dedicated in some way to fixing the widespread problems found in a dysfunctional culture. The skills learned at a training event are still trying to create something great from a place of scarcity—the scarcity of the existing culture (at least the parts that may be dysfunctional). This is the shift a great leader makes from chasing the symptoms of a problem to solving the problem itself. Creating a values-based culture means most of these problems don't arise. The ones that do are effortlessly handled because the values dictate how we treat each other in the process; the values dictate how we identify when people fall in and out of line with acceptable behavior, and it can be openly discussed.

Conventional leadership development gives leaders all kinds of skills and tools to use in an environment that may be rejecting commonsense values. The rejection is simply from not having the navigation tools—the values—to guide us.

Which Companies Live Identifiable Values?

Let's illustrate how values are truly at the center of culture and critical to leadership. I've picked a few organizations that I believe have clearly defined values anyone can see from the way the organizations operate.

Others that do this well include Apple, Amazon, the American Red Cross, and Build-a-Bear. You can google them to research their values.

NASA's values are simple and clear, and they have created a one-sentence values statement and a graphic to reinforce them. You can find these on their website at https://employeeorientation.nasa.gov/main/CoreValues.htm.

NASA

Mission success requires uncompromising commitment to: Safety, Excellence, Teamwork, and Integrity.

Here is how they describe each value:

Safety—NASA's constant attention to safety is the cornerstone upon which we build mission success. We are committed, individually and as a team, to protecting the safety and health of the public, our team members, and those assets that the Nation entrusts to the Agency.

Excellence—To achieve the highest standards in engineering, research, operations, and management in support of mission success, NASA is committed to nurturing an organizational culture in which individuals make full use of their time, talent, and opportunities to pursue excellence in both the ordinary and the extraordinary.

Teamwork—NASA's most powerful tool for achieving mission success is a multidisciplinary team of diverse, competent people across all NASA Centers. Our approach to teamwork is based on a philosophy that each team member brings unique experience and important expertise to project issues. Recognition of and openness to that insight improves the likelihood of identifying and resolving challenges to safety and mission success. We are committed to creating an environment that fosters teamwork and processes that support equal opportunity, collaboration, continuous learning, and openness to innovation and new ideas.

Integrity—NASA is committed to maintaining an environment of trust that is built upon honesty, ethical behavior, respect, and candor. Our leaders enable this environment by encouraging and rewarding a vigorous, open flow of communication on all issues, in all directions, among all employees without fear of reprisal. Building trust through ethical conduct as individuals and as an organization is a necessary component of mission success.

Virgin Airlines

1. We think customer
2. We lead the way
3. We do the right thing
4. We are determined to deliver
5. Together we make the difference

With Honor

In my research, this was a clear favorite when it came to a list of values. This veterans group "With Honor" is a new (as of 2017) group with a simple mission: to elect principled, next-generation veterans to public office who will work in a cross-partisan way to create a more effective and less polarized government.

Whether you are Republican, Democrat, or Independent, that mission may appeal to you. After reading that mission, you may find their values to be self-evident:

1. Integrity

I will always speak the truth and prioritize the public interest above my self-interest.

- I will return or give to charity any contributions from sources that I find out taint my integrity.
- I will use the power of my office only for the service of my constituents and my country.

2. Civility

I will respect my colleagues, focus on solving problems, and work to bring civility to politics.

- I will publicly reject and seek to remove any advertisements in support of my campaign that lie about or baselessly attack the character of my opponent.
- I will attend and participate in a cross-partisan veterans caucus.

3. Courage

I will defend the rights of all Americans and have the courage to collaborate across the aisle and find common ground.

- I will meet with someone from an opposing party one-on-one at least once a month.
- I will join with colleagues on both sides of the aisle on at least one piece of major legislation each year, and co-sponsor additional pieces.

Embedded in these With Honor values are actual ways for members to outwardly demonstrate each value (such as supporting legislation from another party as a demonstration of *courage*). Most of what we've seen in recent years is a congressman or senator from your party expressing a similar intent, but it almost sounds like they are saying "I'll cross the aisle if they will." If you're familiar with game theory, it's at its best in government: people acting in their own self-interest in spite of intentions expressed otherwise. Is that authentic? No. No wonder those branches of government have consistently low approval ratings. We all smell the B.S. If you have an ounce of impartiality, you see both parties behave that way when it comes to working together.

While this isn't a referendum on politics, it is one on leadership. Obviously, there's a connection to what we all openly observe regularly happening in Washington, D.C.

Culture Is Not Separate From Values

Where do most companies disconnect values and culture? Simply put, in Western culture, pretty much every company has something they call set of values. They come in the package deal with a mission and vision. Who made that rule? It doesn't come with your incorporation or LLC paperwork.

They exist because they have benefit if done appropriately. An overused biblical quote (Proverbs 29:18) reads "Where there is no vision, the people will perish." I find that to be a little dramatic, but it's worth noting that teams with dysfunction often pinpoint "lack of vision" as a reason why work may be inconsistent, mistake prone, or otherwise ineffective.

If *safety* is truly an important construct of effective and successful work, it should be a focus, not an assumption.

If *respect* is important to the culture of a particular team, don't assume that the word on a poster means people are carrying it out. It must be somehow actively visible.

Where marriages and partnerships sometimes fail is where we stop focusing on *love* and *appreciation.* It is assumed—and you might think, "Of course I love him or her, and of course he or she knows it." Of course, if that effort wanes over the years, the bond, trust, and love wanes with it.

How Can Values Steer the Culture in the Leader's Absence?

Leaders set the tone. They don't have to be perfect; they just need to be consistent and own their mistakes and acknowledge when they broke a rule, just like everyone else.

We've all told a lie before. We've all violated a value of ours at some time in our lives. It's normal to step outside of a value; it's called a mistake. Having open values means you easily correct yourself. Think of a compass: it may not direct you, but it's used much more to correct you as you stray—so you don't stray too far. This is a Zen idea: when you have strayed, like mindfulness, simply realize you have strayed, and you are automatically back . . . it's when you don't pay attention to the stray that you remain strayed from that value.

Values matter.

When a leader has modeled the way effectively, the values can be more easily carried out when the leader isn't there to drive them. This is how people are on the same page even if work expectations may be muddied.

Modeled values can serve as an example even after people leave the team. From the earlier example with Last-Minute Monica, her group of newly-groomed managers clearly demonstrated how the leader's values can steer the culture, even after her people moved on to start their own groups. She was so adept at putting her people's success above everything, her leaders learned that value from her and carried it out very well. They excelled at treating people with respect, endlessly teaching them skills, supporting their successes, and encouraging their hearts to always reach higher achievement. The higher achievement happened, too. When they opened up their own offices and recruited their own teams, that part was very successful even if some other parts weren't. It was interesting to see how new managers were so much like the leaders who groomed them, for better or worse.

How to Model the Way

When I first meet a team that will be dependent on me for leadership in any form—and this can be a kid's basketball team, a group of clinical educators, or even a senior leadership team—I make it a point to identify what's important for us to function. In any of these examples, I first identify common and important values. This is because these values are authentic to what's in my heart and usually align with theirs. When properly expressed, others will identify these values and understand how my behavior is driven by them.

I'll express a value to any of these groups. For instance, *courage*. I'll usually communicate it something like this:

"Courage is very important to me. That means I'll tell you something important even when I'm scared of how you'll react or what you'll think of me for saying it. It also means I'll always try to stick my neck out for the success of this group. I want you to be great, and that means I'll have to grow a little to learn about you. I'm ready to do that. I may not always do that well, but I'll try to correct myself whenever I make a mistake."

Now that the team knows this, if I am reluctant to carry anything out, I can say that I want to be courageous and do it anyway even if it's not perfect, so I'll accept—and expect—their input, help, and support. More importantly, when I see someone doing something outside of their comfort zone, I can recognize it: "That took guts. I'm really glad you had the courage to do that . . . " and express some form of support for what I just saw.

Most importantly, something magical happens when you do this. As a leader sets that tone and models that way, it continues to echo when they aren't even there to do it. Groups where that standard of *courage* is expressed and supported tend to act with courage more freely. They are empowered to do so. Last-Minute-Monica's managers were echoes of her values (i.e., what was most important to her based on her actions); they carried out what was actually important to her in the best way they could. Her true values were their compass when they were on their own.

Teams that have depended on me tend to demonstrate courage, transparency, openness, enthusiasm, sincerity, and other values that are important to me. It's taken me several years to actually figure out why. Best of all, they usually do this to the extent that people who observe that team tell me about it. That means the teams are doing it mostly because they see me do it, talk about it, recognize it in others, and acknowledge that I'm imperfect at it and that others can be, too. It's not about being 100 percent in that value; it's the habit of righting the ship when you stray. If you stray and ignore it, others may see it; when nothing is done to reconnect to that value and get back on track, people view that as inconsistent, insincere, and even sometimes hypocritical.

This is somewhat counterintuitive. We assume relationships between leaders and teams are eroded and damaged when leaders stray. In reality, most of the damage is done with how the leader *responds* to such a stray from values. It's like when a politician or public figure does something embarrassing. Usually, the denial and insincere behavior after the fact does more damage than the incident alone did. Yet, when a leader is genuinely contrite about an error and sincere about how to correct what they did (or not do it again), it's gone by the next news cycle with minimal consequence.

Have you ever called a leader hypocritical, even just in your mind? We've all seen inconsistent or hypocritical behavior and thought this. Someone may have even thought that about you, if you've strayed from a value and not addressed it.

If You Have Modeled the Way, You Are Easy to Follow

Ultimately, when a leader has modeled the way and openly followed the compass of values, others will do the same. Just like when a manufacturing line in a factory has clear standards for safety and work, there isn't a need for someone to stand over them repeating such things. When boundaries and standards of behavior are clear in the workplace values, a leader's work does itself.

When a leader is away from their team—such as at a meeting or on vacation—are they tethered to their team and the team's needs? Are the daily emergencies emailed constantly to the leader? When values are clear, values are running the show and the leader doesn't *have* to as much. A vacation can be an actual vacation. A true test of this in action is if a leader goes away for a week, is that team motivated to excel in their absence, or are they worried about getting work done? Granted, values aren't the only driver of a team's functionality and success, but they absolutely dictate the culture no matter who is in the room.

I once took a trip to Europe and discussed some of the expectations of the vacation with my team. I asked them if it were possible for me not to have to work while I was away. I didn't ask my leader for this permission. I asked my team. They were more than happy to rise to the occasion. This amazing group of people engaged in the planning for this week with enthusiasm and were excited to take on some of the tasks. One of the factors driving behavior was that they wanted things to get done better *without* me than *with* me. I saw this as an honor, so I set it as a fun goal.

In all honesty, I cared more about them showing off their independence than I did about how it might make me look. The result was an outstanding week of productivity; I received many pictures of all the fun they had. People emerged from that week to demonstrate leadership initiative that I hadn't previously expected. How do I know? They demonstrated values we all agreed were important to us: courage, high effort, transparency, support for each other over competition, and loyalty to each other. They all wanted each other to be successful, and they all acted courageously and enthusiastically to see it happen. They were motivated and guided by things already inside of them. I was so proud of them, and I never let them forget it while we worked together.

It's clear by now that values are the bottom line—maybe you haven't seen these concepts described quite this way, but you've experienced the results of good and bad values, your own and others'. Choose, demonstrate, and reinforce your values well for your workplace and team and you will not only be *easy* to follow, you will build an *enjoyable* and productive culture.

Next, let's talk about how to choose your values.

CHAPTER 5

Live by the Code of Your Values

When you understand how important communicating and demonstrating values are to your leadership, how do you identify what your own personal values are? Some of them are easy and obvious, but some are not.

What Are Your Values?

With every coaching or consulting interaction I do, an important measure of success is making sure I leave the individual with knowledge and understanding that will make a sustainable, significant difference in how they experience their work or personal life. Sometimes this is simply taking a look at "before and after."

I want the same for anyone who reads this book.

One of those takeaways is some methods for identifying your values. Another is what follows on how to take advice—which includes everything I'm suggesting in this book.

As a teenager, I learned from my mother how to think about and accept (or reject) advice in a way that has helped me immensely in my coaching and my own leadership.

Teenagers are biologically wired to exert their independence, so her advice got harder to take when I reached that time in my life. She told me, "I'm gonna give you a lot of advice. All the time. It all comes from a place of love. Do me a favor: instead of bristling or arguing over the merit of it, simply take what you need and discard the rest or save it for later . . . even if you take nothing. Once in a while, you may actually hear something you can use."

I always valued that approach. What that motherly advice allowed me to do was be a better listener. I learned to just let the advice come and go without the need to resist it, feel embarrassed, or argue with her. I just listened. I disregarded some advice as incorrect, inappropriate, or even insane. Sometimes, I really got something of value (even if I never admitted it). This arrangement didn't stop as I became an adult. In fact, I have found this attitude to be of greater value as I get older. Listen, take what you need, discard the rest.

This approach to receiving advice can work wonders in the workplace. I'd like to pass that attitude on to you as you learn more about leadership and as you read this book. Some of the things discussed in this book may be easier to adopt than others. Take what's valuable to you. What can you use that may make your professional or personal life better? What will make you easy to follow? Discard the rest. Maybe you'll find something of importance in it, some day in the future. Maybe someone you care about will benefit from it.

Work-Life Balance, Family, and Authenticity

Part of your authenticity as a leader is the emphasis you place on work-life balance—in the big-picture view, how important your life outside work is. This is a big part of many people's values, and it also reflects the attitudes of the generations who share the workplace.

In many twenty-first century business environments, the idea of work-life balance has grown in importance. Like a tree, the branches of this idea are spreading in many directions, but they are part of the same intention: a happy workforce is an engaged one.

A couple decades ago, members of Generation X—loosely defined by Pew Research as those born from 1965-1979—began to break from traditional corporate norms in the workplace. Growing up with working parents and a lot of autonomy, they brought the value of independence to the workforce and marked the beginning of diminishing job loyalty. In the twenty-first century, staying in a job for longer than four years is a rare feat. Just three decades ago, in a more traditional work environment, 30-40 years in the same work environment was much more common.

At the center of this independence from the job is work-life balance. A tenet of traditional corporate life was working long hours, hoping those extra hours and that loyal dedication could be cashed out in the future for some big promotion or other benefit. In doing so, people missed out on soccer games, recitals, plays, and other important family happenings. The proof? In 1990, a new father would be likely to ask for more hours, a promotion, or some other increase in work in order to support the family. Since about 2010, new fathers ask for paternity leave.

Priorities have shifted. People debate whether or not this is for the better. I am not afraid to say I absolutely support people's commitments to be with their family over job commitments.

Parenting is more important than profit, right?

No matter what beliefs you have, in some way or another you only have this one life, and it goes by in a blink. Some figure out how to have it all—a strong family and an abundant career. Others act like there is a choice, that you can only have one at the expense of the other.

Did you know you don't have to choose, and you don't have to be privileged to have both? I also absolutely believe that a strong, healthy family life *is* an abundant career. And vice versa. You can't actually do one without the other. Like two sides to a coin. Having one without the other is a false perception, just like you can't have a coin with only one side. Here's why.

I once heard a consultant training a group of leaders about conflict resolution. He was giving some scripts and tactics, and everyone was largely accepting what he was teaching. Then he said something that struck me: "All bets are off with this stuff when it comes to spouses and teenagers. None of this stuff applies to life at home." Are you kidding me? He just basically said this stuff doesn't work. Being good at resolving conflict is only useful when important things are at stake. I can't think of a more important arena to navigate conflict than your family. I can say with the utmost confidence that living my values has meant my personal relationships—including during times of conflict—are deeply enriching. In relationships with my loved ones, this matters most.

The leader you are is someone with values. Those values may or may not be clear to those around you, yet. What's important is that the leader connects with family, peers, other leaders, children, and anyone who depends on the leader. You'll find that there is no value that has meaning for employees but not your family.

I've heard couples argue in some personal circles and have occasionally heard one say, "Don't talk to me like I'm one of your employees." What's at play there is a break in authenticity. It's someone wearing the manager hat that doesn't fit at work, and it *really* doesn't fit at home.

Authenticity is that connection between what's inside our hearts and our heads with what's easy for others to perceive on the outside.

When we're trying hard to use some skill we learned to win an argument or influence someone, it can be blatantly out of character. People who know you best can most easily see this and will most likely call you out for doing or saying something that isn't natural for you.

Think of the person you care about most in your life—or someone to whom you are very close and trust the most. Do you exist with that person conflict-free? Of course not. In fact, you may have more conflict with her/him than any other human. Why is that? It's because the single best way to build trust is to successfully navigate conflict with someone. It's that experience of disagreeing, sharing what's in your heart or mind, risking being ridiculed because it's different than what's in the other person's mind, and coming out clean on the other end. That person who is close to you—you have conflict with them, but you know those rough waters and how to navigate them. You know what buttons not *to push and usually make a genuine attempt to avoid them. That may be imperfect, but that's the biggest contributor to whom we trust. It's the experience of being vulnerable, showing emotion . . . being authentic.*

Values Exercises

Step one in being authentic is knowing what your values are.

Your values will unlock much of your success in any leadership role you have. How you go about finding them is a deeply personal and individual quest.

Having a leadership role in your work isn't for everybody, but understanding how to be a leader benefits everyone. I can give you a couple ways to arrive at a set of values that truly resonates with you.

Commit yourself to follow through with one or both of these exercises. Not later, not tomorrow, now. If you are someplace where that's not possible, stop reading and pick this up when you can do it. I can't emphasize this enough. It's a simple enough thought experiment, but you want to be writing or typing while you do it.

Method One: Self-Guided Discovery

Start by answering this one fill-in-the-blank question. This will get you to one or two of your most core values. While it's okay to have a list, most people find that there is one or two that really guide them more than any others; just as a compass has many marks and directions, there is one needle. Where does it point?

_____ *is very important to me.*

The blank is some behavior you think you exhibit well (or want to exhibit well) and that you wish you saw more of in others.

Live by the Code of Your Values

It can be anything. It can be *teamwork, assertiveness, discipline*. Anything. Don't worry that this needs to be your absolute, core value—this exercise is meant to help you find that by starting with what you can clearly see. Now say it in your mind as a full statement. As you say it, is there a new word that pops in your head that also wants to be heard? You may start by saying, "Teamwork is very important to me," and a voice in your mind blurts out, "Kindness . . . can't have teamwork without kindness!!!" That's okay. That means you've invited your values to speak up.

Now take one of the words. Here's where you get to revert to your two-year-old self and ask a series of whys until you can't answer anymore. If your word was kindness, ask "Why is kindness so important to me?" (or) "Why does kindness matter?" Answer that question, then ask *why* again. Repeat.

An interesting thing happens here. We start to really understand our commitments. In engineering, this is the process by which experts in the Lean and Six Sigma processes get to the root cause of a problem. They identify a problem and keep asking why it's happening until there is a *why* that has no answer or needs data collection to answer it. This helps people get to the problem itself rather than just chasing a symptom of the problem.

Take the above example where the easy answer is *teamwork*. The answer isn't always easy to find. When you find it, you will understand things about yourself you hadn't realized—and you'll be easier to follow as a result. Watch this play out:

1. Why is teamwork so important?

   Because we get more done as a team.

2. Why is that important?

People genuinely have more fun when we're working together and getting more done.

(There were two things to ask why about: fun and getting more done . . . so we split it.)

3. A. Why is it important to get more done?

Job security—we're being productive, we're feeling good about our satisfied customers.

B. Why is it important to have job security?

It's good for morale, stress levels, and income/livelihood.

4. A. Why is it important to have fun?

People will want to be here. Friendships can be fostered. Life is enriched.

B. Okay, why is it important to want to be here for friendships and enriched life?

Because work, like all of life, should be fun.

What you've effectively done here is connected to your purpose. By simply having the discipline to drill down from some buzzword to what that word really means for you, you've tapped into an authenticity that can be freely shared.

The rule of thumb here is that you should keep asking *why* until you get some emotional response.

Keep asking why until you get an emotional response.

No matter how emotional you consider yourself to be, when you land on one of these correctly, you'll be able to feel it with an emotion. That means your answer carried with it a deep meaning for you—it's a true value.

Some leaders will say, "We need better teamwork," and just tell people to start working together. Like that's all they needed. "Oh!" they reply. "You mean, '*work*' '*together*'? Oh, I had no idea . . . thanks for that great advice!" (Yes, there is sarcasm there . . .)

It's not that simple—it's *even simpler*. Yes. Simpl*er*.

With this exercise, a leader gets to say, "We need better teamwork; we'll get more done for our customers, but we'll also be having more fun together, and that's what is important to me." Can you get a sense of how different people will view that slightly deeper statement? It's no longer teamwork for the sake of teamwork. It could mean something important to people now. Watch their own compass light up. They don't need a class in difficult conversations to collectively want to have more fun together. This is why expressing values changes everything.

This exercise can help you be clear about who you are trying to be. It can close gaps in perceptions and communication and eliminate blind spots in your relationships. Think back to that analogy about how the quarterback is throwing a pass and someone else has to catch it. Throw a ball that is easy to catch. Be easy to follow. Expressing teamwork as a value in that way is like throwing a ball that's easy to catch.

Knowing Your Values Makes Them Your Default

Having clear values means you are not only more likely to adhere to them when you aren't paying attention, but so are others who depend on you for leadership. These are called **default moments**. When you are under stress, the biology of anxiety and adrenaline pump blood away from your higher brain function. This literally means that when you are under any kind of duress, you are dumber. If you don't believe me, think of the last argument or interview you had. It wasn't until about 15 minutes after it was over when you suddenly remembered the thing you wished you had said. As your hormones normalize, your higher brain functions return to you. That takes about 15 minutes.

Your default moments are the behaviors that take over when you're not really focused on how you're performing; you're just focused on the task at hand. When you're in the habit of being open about your values and behaviors, the distance between values and the behaviors in your default moments will shorten. I've witnessed this in myself, my loved ones, and in leaders I've coached.

So try it a few more times. Fill in the blank (there are four here, but do as many or as few as you need):

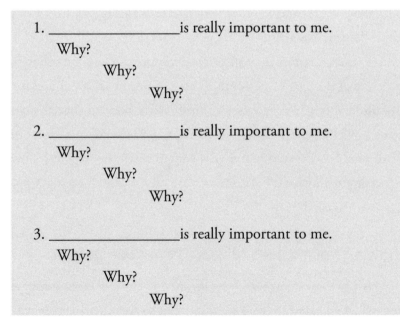

1. _____is really important to me.
   Why?
        Why?
           Why?

2. _____is really important to me.
   Why?
        Why?
           Why?

3. _____is really important to me.
   Why?
        Why?
           Why?

4. _____is really important to me.

   Why?

         Why?

                 Why?

Method Two: Find Your Values Online

1000minds Decision Making is decision-making software. Landing on values can be a difficult task. Some days you may come up with a different set of words than other days.

1000minds (1000minds.com) is an online suite of tools and processes for ranking, prioritizing, or choosing between alternatives when multiple objectives or criteria need to be considered simultaneously. In other words, 1000minds is for performing "Multi-Criteria Decision Analysis" and "Conjoint Analysis" (aka "Choice Modelling"). Depending on the application, 1000minds can also help users think about the value for money of alternatives and allocate budgets or other scarce resources. 1000minds implements the PAPRIKA method—an acronym for **P**otentially **A**ll **P**airwise **R**an**K**ings of all possible **A**lternatives—to determine the relative importance of the criteria for the decision at hand, based on the preferences of decision-makers.

Use this QR code to access an assessment or go to 1000minds.com/go/valuesassessment1. It will take you a few minutes, but this is an important exercise and it will help you land on which values are truly most important.

The quiz will ask you to make choices based on preferred groupings. You'll see two short lists of values, and you'll be asked which set of values more represents you. Even if neither one is a great fit, it will ask you which is better. You'll compare several lists this way with simple either-or selections and you'll be presented with a short list that most likely expresses which values are most important to you.

Having the value is great. Showing the value is leadership.

Once you have a few values you really like and you can easily express a *why* that moves you, this is where you do the work that is really meaningful. Once you have a value—"I value _____"—now you must answer these next questions:

How **do you value it?** This is decidedly different from asking *why*. If you value courage, how do you show that? You can seize moments to express courage when you feel hesitation.

Since it's your value, it's your most natural way to behave. It's more work to hide or conceal it, which is sometimes done unconsciously. Most importantly, let others know this is what you value. It's likely they will understand it, and even like it if it's close to one of their own values. You're now learning what leading effortlessly is. You're being easy to follow. Here's another way to approach it:

In order to practice _____ (insert value), I must _____.

Where the blank is an action you can remind yourself to do more.

But here's the unsung hero of values: ***How* do you recognize it in others?**

When you see an important value like *courage* in others, you are now more likely to say to them, "Hey, that took courage; good job." Or if that value is *teamwork,* "You're really having fun, I'm glad you're such a great teammate." This is a level of recognition to which people respond very favorably. It's authentic *and* it's aligned to important things, like all the *whys* discovered in the previous exercise.

Now you've given someone recognition and, more importantly, the encouragement to repeat that effort. That's their emotional payoff for doing something difficult (like their job!). When we fail to provide teams and individuals with the emotional payoff, motivation can fade quickly. Attitudes like, "This is a thankless job," and "No one ever notices hard work around here," exist when leaders do a poor job at recognizing values in action. Small bonuses, free coffee, and other "perks" fall short of this payoff. Most organizations offer them, and think they are properly rewarding people because they've spent money. Even when they offer such things, why do people still feel underappreciated? I think you have your answer.

So here's the most straightforward way I can urge you to get value from this book: apply what you learn from the following exercise.

How to Recognize a Value Demonstrated by Your Team

1. Find a value by saying, "_____ is important to me," and the blank you fill in is your starting value.

2. Ask *why* that word is important, then ask why again with your new answer, and keep repeating the why question with each answer until you can't go anymore. *That's* your true value, in that last, emotional statement.

3. You are free to do this for just one value, or for a few. I suggest keeping it under six; beyond that, they start blurring together.

4. Decide *how* you will value this value. That just means identifying what parts of your natural behavior you are now going to set free. What will you express?

5. Decide how you will recognize this in others.

"Your candle loses nothing when it lights another."

—James Keller

Item number five above—deciding how you will recognize this in others—may prove to be critically useful in your world. When you recognize a positive value in others, you have engaged in the strongest form of workforce development: *culture change.*

Organizations often view culture change as some boulder to push up a mountain; it's a colossal undertaking. How do you get one person to change? It is not easy or even really possible. How about getting everyone in a company to change? It's that much harder. Yet that's a common view of culture change. It's also the one that only serves to further alienate a team. After all, who *wants* to be changed or indoctrinated into some kind of groupthink?

Most teams reject efforts to change their culture, even if unconsciously. No one likes hearing they are part of a problem they only see in others, and they like advice on how to behave even less. On the other hand, who wants to connect with their coworkers at a deep level, where we all know we are doing the right thing and supporting each other's best interests? I think we all do. The difference is profound.

Leaders Don't Have to Be the Expert in Everything

Leaders don't have to be able to do everything their team can do. In most cases, the team has expertise that simply isn't broadly shared. When a leader can't effectively do something that someone on the team can do, some people see that as a problem. It shouldn't be. An executive director of surgery may be a surgeon, but if they are a neurosurgeon by trade, there should be no expectation that they should be able to perform vascular surgery effectively. A foreman doesn't need to know how to operate all the machinery or tools in use for a project.

Where a leader absolutely must walk the talk is when it comes to values. That will translate to any environment. It's a language common to every industry. It's effortless to support and enable certain behaviors when you're actively and openly demonstrating them.

Take any one value from the previous section. Now ask this question and honestly work to come up with tangible answers:

"If my team started behaving with (*value*), what will change?"

List up to three things that would improve if somehow everyone was in lockstep with that behavior.

1.

2.

3.

This exercise may seem simple and benign, even obvious—but there is a real benefit. What if you shared this value *and* the benefits of the value in action with your team, as individuals or as a group? How do you think the team may respond to this? What if you shared this, not to push it out heavy-handedly (not *mandatory*), but to just open a discussion with them to see if they agree? Would they add anything to or omit anything from the list? Would they agree on the importance of the value? Would they want to come up with a slightly different word?

Imagine the results of that discussion. You'll experience a high level of buy-in around some shared behaviors. The conversation could get a little awkward and uncomfortable, but this is the single most powerful way to shape your organization's culture today. Once you've had the conversation, benefitting from that buy-in is so effortless, it's automatic.

This method of culture change, if done with an open heart and mind, is not pushing a boulder up a mountain; it's just being the mountain. There is no boulder.

How Do You Value Your Values?

If you have not *communicated* values, you may be okay with "winging it." That means just trying your best to be a good and virtuous person each and every day. Most leaders have done that their whole careers with varying success. We all do that on some level. The problem is, the leaders and coworkers for whom you have the least respect might also be winging it daily.

If someone asks you what your values are, you may grasp at the first things you remember from Sunday school or your parents and say something like, "Honesty, um, and integrity," but those words alone ring empty. Have you ever caught someone in a lie, then at some point later heard them state that they either appreciate honesty or honesty is important to them? They lose credibility in your eyes. When values are openly expressed, there is no hiding. Valuing honesty and then being caught in the whitest of lies means you have to talk about it. It may be awkward, but it keeps the trust and support strong. No one is hiding.

Your values are like a compass or a map. It doesn't mean you're always virtuous; it means when you lose your way you can know where to find it again.

I value acting with courage. I'm not always courageous. In fact, I could call myself a chicken many more times than I would call myself courageous. It's when I catch myself slipping that I know it's important to me to act with courage and try hard to find my way.

"Values are like fingerprints. . . . you leave 'em all over everything you do."

–Elvis Presley

Your values should always be yours. Sharing them is fine, and also necessary; it's how others can most easily identify with you. It's how you are easy to follow. Fundamentally, we all have many of them in common.

CHAPTER 6

Leading Effortlessly;
Being Easy to Follow

If you are easy to follow, many of the difficult elements of leadership become easier—or even effortless. Through your values, you can build a culture where some common team problems don't (or can't) develop. And the team can behave in a manner they know will please you, even when you are not there.

Identifying your values shows everyone what's truly important. When you invite your team's buy-in concerning these values, and if you work with them to choose the team's values, you and your team will understand each other better and see each other's authenticity more clearly.

Why Do People Follow Values Over Skills?

People follow values over skills because they relate to them, agree with them, and recognize that they give meaning to life and to their efforts at work—they are ultimately the reasons *why* we are all here. Connecting with someone's values can be an emotional, impactful experience. Skills don't connect people or impact people at an emotional level, typically. They just aren't important enough.

There is magic in declaring the values that are important to you—verbally, through your actions, or in writing. The moment you express that something like *honesty* is important, honesty becomes a more active part of your daily practice. Others hold you accountable just by seeing you and don't have to say anything. It's the accountability of no accountability. It's automatic. Clear values guide us in the way our habits do; we barely have to think about them.

Values become not only visible but central to the work when they are recognized; no one needs a class or conference to achieve that. It doesn't even need to show up on your company's budget. This is the only leadership development that truly works—and it's free.

This level of leading is effortless. It transparently aligns actions and intentions and enables others to align with you. It allows you to have the impact you seek on those who depend on you, workplace teams and loved ones alike. Leading effortlessly with values has no particular form. You don't even create it. It's already there. The effort may come in identifying the values, living the values, and recognizing them in others—all of which require a level of being present, or mindfulness. You need to have that list of values in your mind when an opportunity presents itself.

Why Does Learning Skills and a Conventional Leadership Development Approach Make You Harder to Follow?

How have you experienced leadership development where you work?

Leaders are quite commonly given a skill to learn. This comes in many forms. Sometimes it's their boss forwarding a link to an article. Other times, leaders are given direction as part of an annual goal to attend a conference or class. Other forms this can take are more ad hoc; an organization schedules a class or retreat and brings in something timely and/or short term.

Leaders will usually learn whatever this is and try it on with their teams with little context. It's like showing up one day, and suddenly sporting a moustache or a hat. People who are close to you may ask you about it immediately. Others will wait patiently until you leave the room to ask others if they noticed the change, and everyone discusses what they think of it. Group dynamics won't usually play favorably when it comes to this. Generally, people are far more likely to commiserate and banter over things they don't like than talk about changes they love.

As an example, let's say a leader reads a book on conflict resolution. There are many great resources about how to resolve conflict or have difficult conversations; they mostly help with what to say to an adversary and why to say it. Most of the existing work in this area is based on very sound psychology. It's good. The problem is when the leader brings it to the environment that made the conversations difficult to begin with. This new sense of purpose and smooth phrasing to navigate the conversation is no more useful than that new moustache. To some, even if your intentions are totally pure, you will seem less authentic. This includes when you improve your own lousy habits and behavior—and it can get tricky.

I once worked with a manager who had such low scores on a multi-rater assessment (a 360 review, where people can anonymously rate their boss) in the area of trust, she wanted to quit. Conventional wisdom would be to get her to change her ways immediately with some actions that are associated with trust. The problem is that her sudden changes in behavior would be perceived as inauthentic. People didn't see her as sincere to begin with. This quickly becomes a catch-22: she can't stay in her current state, yet honest efforts to improve would further erode her standing.

This may be an unusual example, but it expresses the cautionary tale: skill development alone does not make you a better leader; it can do more damage than you think.

Learning Skills? Old Habits Die Hard

Why is change so difficult? There is no accurate data on how much money is spent on change management training and consultants, but it's a lot. William Bridges has a body of work in this area that has stood the test of time. One of his basic ideas is that it's not change people resist, it's the transition. He describes the difference between the two as change is an event, and transition is how we psychologically adapt to the event. While lots of planning and strategy focus on the change itself, the people who must carry it out are largely disregarded and yet they are the most important part of the initiative. They hold the key to its success or failure.

What this means on a deeper level is that we have our habits and how we behave is one of them. We all behave within a certain set of boundaries. If a change that must occur is clear and our role exists within these boundaries, it's easier for us to adapt. However, if we see this change as interfering with our values (i.e., the things we think of as important), we will resist change overtly, covertly, or sometimes even unconsciously.

When some leaders want to drive change, authoritarianism sometimes kicks in, and common explanations include "the bus is leaving the station with or without you, so be on it." Few things make it harder for a leader to be followed than forcibly telling others what is in their best interest. When leaders can connect a change to what's important to the person or the team (rather than convincing them *why* it's important and hoping they get it), it goes further.

Learning Skills? Attachment to Results

A very common part of being a leader is accountability to results. Inherent in this approach is to "drive results." This may even show up on some lists of corporate values. Driving results isn't really a value. Your values, however, can naturally drive results if they are aligned.

Driving results implies there is resistance. When you are driving results, there is some level of extra effort described (it's not called "getting results" for a reason), and also implicit is that if you're not putting in this effort, results won't happen; ergo, results must be driven, pushed, or whatever.

Imagine a strong rope tied to the wall of a building. Pulling the rope actually gets an equal amount of resistance in the opposite reaction. Yet you may be pulling on such a rope thinking "Imagine if I wasn't pulling so hard, it would be flying in the other direction!" No it wouldn't.

If you don't pull the rope attached to the wall, it's still there, and it's still the same length. Driving results can sometimes mean a leader is leading too far out in front of the organization.

Attachment to results detaches you from the people. Driving results takes you away from growing or supporting the people, who in turn drive the results. Are you stepping on your people to drive results as "musts" and "mandatories"?

Learning Skills? I Learned Conflict Resolution, but No One Else Speaks This Language

When someone learns to speak the language of conflict resolution, it's a strong skill. Taking that skill back to an environment where existing boundaries, values, and use of language have made conflict the norm is largely ineffective. It's why months after this skill was learned (or the training was completed), there may be no difference in the nature of conflict in the environment. It's a waste.

If a leader focuses on the *causes* of unproductive conflict, it's more complicated, but a far better option—call it root-cause analysis. When a leader can learn why conflict is a problem on the team, that becomes a much easier endeavor. Rather than trying to get a person to act differently than their natural reaction to things, rather than giving people tools and hoping they all use them consistently and fairly, the leader with a Zen attitude knows that conflict is healthy. Instead of resisting it, support it.

Tools for managing conflict are usually geared toward ending or diffusing it. How about making conflict okay? Some great work has been written previously around supporting "well-managed conflict" in the workplace. When conflict is encouraged, people work through it much differently than making it akin to an argument where one person inevitably ends the interaction with "Let's agree to disagree." That solves nothing and does even less for positive relationships.

Learning Skills? What Aboutism; What About My Boss? She or He Doesn't Do This

This is difficult. I work with many leaders, most of whom answer to someone (no matter where you are in the pecking order, you answer to someone, even if it's a spouse). When I offer them support around specific needs like "Here's a better way to handle X next time it happens," a common response is, "If that's so good, how come my boss doesn't do that?" This is one of the toughest parts of being a developing leader; once again this is an example where learning leadership can do damage where none was intended. When a leader begins to really learn what makes good supportive behavior and what makes destructive behavior, they get to view themselves with that lens in hopes to be a better person. As a consequence, they also get to view others with this lens. Usually, people who learn about leadership first notice flaws in their leaders before they consider flaws in themselves. It may be happening as you read this book. It can be troublesome to relationships.

This is one place where all the effort and money spent on training a leader commonly falls flat. If they don't perceive people around them putting in the same effort—and especially their own leader—it can be deflating; at the very least, it's not supportive. If a child learns something at school and sees their own parents acting counter to it, a barrier to that learning is erected.

Most of these issues speak to the environment where they exist, rather than the issue itself. That's on purpose. Clearly defined values are a way to build the environment where these issues still exist, but their resolution happens more easily as a result of the common ground that understanding values can bring.

Zen and the Art of Leadership

The Zen approach to philosophy or religion has many applications that can benefit your approach to leadership in the twenty-first century workplace, without ascribing to Buddhism. The focus on introspection, meditation, and mindfulness is particularly useful for improving your self-awareness and viewing behavior and events without habitual "filters" or judgments. This practice can help you see where your behavior is aligned to your values and where it isn't.

Mindfulness and Leadership

An emerging (and now very common) part of work-life balance is the practice of mindfulness. This is the process of bringing one's attention to experiences occurring in the present moment. There are multiple practices that dabble in this process, such as meditation and breathing exercises. Mindfulness can be bringing your attention to the rhythm of your breath. It can be just noticing a physical sensation and paying attention to it.

Our minds naturally wander, so this practice is bringing our wandering attention back to that focal point. Why? It's said that the wandering mind, thanks to evolution, serves to protect us from danger; it constantly processes stimuli. In modern times, emotional pain is as much a danger as a saber-toothed tiger was in prehistoric times. Our minds wander to the past to remind us of things we didn't like more than things we did like. This is natural but can be the root of things like PTSD or depression. Our minds wander to the future for the same reason.

A quote often attributed to Lao Tzu applies here: "If you are depressed you are living in the past. If you are anxious you are living in the future. If you are at peace you are living in the present."

This may oversimplify the psychology and neuroscience, but it's been profound enough to guide people for hundreds of years.

In the information age, we're drowning in stimuli about everything *but* the present. Election cycles never end (they are designed to make you anxious about the future) and news is always about what we should be afraid of. (All news stories happened in the past; we can't change them, and they can make us depressed. Technically, watching the news prevents us from being present.) This flow of external stimuli is bigger now than it's ever been.

It's no surprise that the practice of something like mindfulness is making a resurgence. People in all realms are feeling the value of it. Your leadership practice is reflected in this.

You are mindful of your values. When you stray, as all of us sometimes will, you bring your focus back to them. That act transcends any leadership skill you can learn in any class. When others' behaviors stray, you bring their focus back to values. This is a form of *values mindfulness*. You may be overwhelmed with things that take you away from your values. That's okay; just return to them. Living your values is your natural state.

If it's clear that *customer service* is a value of your environment, and you observe a slip in how someone on your team provides that service to others, the conversation around returning to service is an easy one. It's what everyone wants. It's not a "difficult conversation," or a conflict, or reading some script you have about handling a "low performer." The value is your common ground. The discussion is on how you remind yourself of it. With the value in place, adhering to it is effortless; it's easy.

To see how effortless it can be to return to the moment, to be present and mindful, observe small children and how they interact with the world. A close friend who did wonderful work in youth services used to carry a small bag of mini marshmallows. When a 5- or 6-year-old would start to get upset, she would take out the bag and ask, "Wanna catch a marshmallow?" Immediately, any frustration or pain would subside, and the child would have full presence on the new and interesting task. Sometimes all we need is a distraction. It can help if it's sugar based, I'll admit.

Our reaction to things can be bigger than the trigger. Leaving behind that triggering event can be effortless. In the instance of the marshmallow, we can be tricked into this effortless transformation. But what if there is no marshmallow? Could the same kid do the same transformation? What about as adults? Can we escape our frustrations just as easily? Do we need a marshmallow? Or is it as easy as mindfulness?

I once had a mentor tell me that whatever drama I was experiencing that gave me anxiety, frustration, anger, or any negativity, I could effortlessly escape. Her advice was to sit in this moment, then fast-forward one year and ask yourself: In one year, will you even remember it? If you answer no, you gain immediate perspective and realize this event is not that important anymore.

The obvious next thought from the reader's point of view is, "What if the answer is yes?" Well, in that instance, she said if you think you'll remember it in a year, do you think you'd be able to laugh at it? That answer is almost always yes. So, if you can laugh at it in a year, what barrier exists to laughing at it now? There wasn't one. She instructed me to just laugh at it now. That made such a difference. And if the experience is so dramatic that you won't be able to laugh about it in a year, you genuinely deserve the right to mourn and be upset; you may be experiencing something really horrible. If that's the case, experience it and let it pass. But if you can laugh about it in a year, just laugh about it today. This is Zen—next year is now, and anything within you that can come with time, can come now. It's a sort of fast-forward so you gain a "hindsight is 20-20" perspective on the event when it has just happened.

Mindfulness is the practice of returning to the moment. When values are present, it's also how we return to our values—or what's important—when we stray. Our environments make it easy for our focus to stray. Mindfulness returns it to the present. Likewise, the triggers and stresses around us can make our values stray. When the values are clear, we self-adjust in a similar fashion. It's parallel.

What Is Authenticity?

A big challenge I see in circles of middle management exists around the work connecting people to the concept and value of *authenticity*.

I've already written a lot about authenticity, in previous chapters. Often, I'll describe or demonstrate a model of behavior based on this—what authenticity "looks like." A common response is "What if my leader doesn't do this?"

Many seasoned leaders have a natural aversion to self-reflection. It's the belief that the personality that got them to where they are serves them in all areas. High-level leaders realize that, like water, they adapt to fill the needs of the environment; they let go of rigidity (rigidity actually takes more effort). Regardless of the others around you, this experience of authenticity, clarity, and a values-driven life is all about *you* and your development.

If leadership or becoming a better leader could even be considered an act, it could be considered the act of awakening—enlightenment.

Why Should You Always View Leadership Advice or Skills With a Critical Eye?

People who tried some method within the confines of their own circumstances may tell you the same method will be successful in yours.

Don't listen to them! An important part of everyone's development is to take advice from others with a grain of salt.

Recall the first book (or some other resource) you read on leadership. That book may have benefited you greatly. You may have accepted the views of that book like a gospel, to be closely followed. There can be some benefit to that. That is, someone could see some improvement in their business or leadership thanks to that book's influence.

When that same person begins to hunger for more growth and starts reading more books, not all of the information will be in alignment. That person starts to notice there are contradictions, paradoxes, and various inconsistencies.

Strong leaders who haven't read a lot of leadership books may say that leaders are born, not made, while another leader who benefited greatly from reading leadership-related books could argue the opposite.

Popular magazines like *Forbes* and *Harvard Business Review* publish articles that separately support putting the customer at the center of effort and putting the employee at the center of everything. Are they both correct? If you have two centers, they are no longer the center; it's like having two left sides without a right side.

The point is a simple one. Open your critical eye. The ability for a leader to question the usefulness of any advice leads to many other things effortlessly becoming clearer. The critical eye is the one that looks at everything and asks:

Is there more to this than I can see?

Do I need more information? Is there another side to this story?

Whose opinion about this would be different from mine, and why?

The critical eye also opens your mind. It's been said "the mind is like a parachute; it works best when it's open." This quote is attributed to several sources. What's profound about this is it encourages any reader to find the habit of putting up less resistance. Strong leaders find it's far easier to have an open mind and consider fresh views than it is to strictly adhere to anything.

The effortless leader—the one who is easy to follow—has an open mind. Question things, including yourself. Allow others to question how you see things, and they will most likely allow you to do the same to them. This is another way that leaders set the tone. If the leader values the critical eye, people open their own and can see it in others.

Open a critical eye to all resources, including this one, to test how it fits in your circumstances. If you ever decide something doesn't fit, be sure to question if it *should* fit, or if the reason it doesn't fit *now* is because it may require you to grow a little.

How Is Accountability Best Executed?

No one can make you change. Even someone with absolute authority who thinks they can force you to "change, quit, or be fired" still can't change you. I've worked with many leaders who are committed to changing someone so they behave better or perform to a higher level. My message to them is simple: You will never get anyone to change. Period. Not at work, not at home.

Ask yourself if you would have (or ever have in the past) responded favorably to this comment: *"You should work smarter."*

The answer is probably a big "No." What's implicit in that statement is that if you aren't working "smart," you're working "dumb."

In reality, you're working in the smartest way you know how. Someone else's way may or may not be beneficial to you. loading a dishwasher. If you ever want to play a mean trick on two people, ask them to load the dishwasher together. Pause for a moment to think about how that plays out. There are usually competing plans for how to best load it, with bowls, plates, and mugs, all in their special place, which is completely wrong to the other person. Who is right? You may think you are Earth's Supreme Dish Loader, but others have that same self assessment. In reality, both are effective ways. Even if one way gets one or two more plates in, the alternative is still fine. Most workplace and family conflict stems from minor idiosyncrasies like this. Just because a new way is different, it may not be better.

Instead, I suggest a better way for that manager to find change. Rather than engage their employee(s) in conversations around changing or improving, I ask them to build context. While you can't get someone to change, you can show them the context of their actions. When people see clearly the negative impact of their actions, they change. Don't believe me? That's okay, most people don't believe that when I first say it. But they come around when I ask them this question:

> . . . *If there was some habit you had of which you were unaware; something you did with regularity that frustrated and angered anyone who was around you, would you want to know about it, or would you rather just keep doing it?*

Everyone answers yes to that, even if reluctantly. That's right, 100 percent of people I ask that question of eventually land on "Yes, I'd want to know if I was doing something that everyone hated." When I ask why, the response is similar to "So I can do something about it."

This is interesting. Saying that 100 percent of the people I ask this respond similarly says a lot about our need to *self-correct* over our need to *be corrected*. When we find out we're doing something that others genuinely don't like, we stop it; unless we have some other motive to persist—but that is very rare in reality.

Now reverse this exercise. If you saw someone doing something regularly that you know was annoying you and others, would you tell them? People freeze when I ask them this. They know they should say "Yes" based on the previous exercise, but in reality, we don't talk about this with the person doing the annoying thing. I hear people say, "They should know better." Or "I don't want to fight with them. I'm choosing my battles." Immediately this becomes a difficult conversation that you may avoid having altogether.

Honestly, we just established that 100 percent of people would want to know if they were doing something annoying, so they could do something about it. So why would we be afraid to tell someone else if they were doing something annoying? Obviously that person doesn't think it's annoying or they probably wouldn't be doing it.

Note: If you think they knowingly behave this way (i.e., they wake up in the morning and say aloud "I wonder how I can annoy person X today") you are operating from a victim's perspective, and that is not a realistic place from which to lead anyone.

When the leader understands an issue from many angles, they can see something out of character and think to themselves, "If it were me, I'd want someone to let me know I do that . . . ." That leader can then approach that person about how they would want to be told. If values (like courage or integrity) are clear on both sides, self-correction is easy.

Trying to change a person is usually met with defensiveness or another form of resistance. However, presenting the context, i.e., the impact of their behavior on other people or on the work itself, people will change—but only if the other people or work is important. If it's not, the more important conversation comes up. This self-adjustment is natural and normal when there is clarity around what is important and what brings us away from what's important.

How Is Making Problems "No Problem" the Best Way to Give Feedback?

This is where we start to fully understand what being easy to follow is about.

Your values are a start. When they are openly visible, accessible, and shared, they are the sky in which others can soar freely.

Problems occur naturally. Peter Drucker famously said, "Only three things happen naturally in organizations: friction, confusion, and underperformance. Everything else requires leadership."

No leader wants to hear this, but that doesn't make it untrue: the leader is the owner of—and therefore the *cause* of—the environment where friction, confusion, and underperformance naturally happen.

Just as it takes no effort to erode relationships and trust, it is also no effort to maintain them.

When Conflict Isn't Conflict

Imagine the conflict that happens in an atmosphere of no conflict. This is the environment where opinions can vary and people are not attached to them, one way or another. There is no fighting, only listening to understand. The environment that encourages conflict and speaking freely with an understanding of the values can actually have more conflict than other environments, but conflict isn't a problem—it becomes something else, something productive. Is it conflict at all? It's not resisted or avoided. It's encouraged, so it's nothing to fear. Some organizations call this well-managed conflict. Others call it "discussion." How novel.

These paradoxes might seem hard to understand, so I encourage you to not understand them at all, at least not in a way that is taxing. Make it effortless.

When Feedback Is Unnecessary

This is making problems into no problem. Is feedback in your organization difficult and sometimes awkward? Imagine a workplace where the feedback of "no feedback" is the norm. While you may cringe at an environment where no one is telling each other how to improve, imagine that workplace where people knew clearly what was needed and inherently wanted to improve, seeking out tools (training or learning) and/or resources (each other) to achieve this.

Do people really need to be told to do something better? Do you? If your results dip or waver, does a boss really need to tell you to improve? Is the best accountability from a boss, or from yourself?

Imagine you are walking on a path, and up ahead you see a snake coiled and ready to strike. Your body immediately goes into fight-or-flight mode. All of the hormonal precursors start coursing through your system. You feel the physical symptoms of fight or flight; you are nervous, anxious, ready to keep yourself safe in this dangerous situation. As you approach the snake, you see that it's just a rope. Are you still afraid? Of course not.

Imagine a similar situation playing out at work. You see some difficult situation ahead, like a tough meeting or some interaction you find unpleasant. As you view it, you have all the similar hormonal precursors; you feel anxious, nervous, and fearful of what's coming. The same components of self-protection unfold.

Most people will do what it takes to avoid that feeling, that dread of an unpleasant interaction caused by your own performance.

Teamwork, Transition, and Respect

Every leadership situation is unique, depending on what is happening in the organization—is it growing, is it struggling to stay in the black, is it adapting to an acquisition? All of these things contribute to the uniqueness of your needs and how your values should be expressed—not to mention the other people involved.

Start-ups are exciting cultures. Each successful start-up struggles with growth and I've helped many founders transition to CEOs. Think of a start-up like a speedboat. It can move quickly on a market trend and respond rapidly to change. Like a speedboat, it's fast and agile. This flexibility is critical in order to take root as a viable company. As the company grows, it can no longer be a speedboat; it's bigger. A bigger boat loses some of that agility. In a lot of ways, an aircraft carrier moves faster than a speedboat, but changing course is no longer as easy.

As a start-up grows, they often experience the frustration of resembling a larger organization. An aircraft carrier can't act like a speedboat and will look bad trying to, and the same is true in an organization. A start-up founder makes an important transition when they make the first changes as the company grows. When a founder is first hiring for a start-up, they'll hire anyone who "sees what they see." This is important in a small company; the founder is essentially multiplying herself/himself through the effort of others. However, a homogenous workforce is not a good idea, once the company starts to grow. Founders become CEOs when they realize it's okay to bring on differing opinions.

> # Start-up founders become CEOs when they realize it's okay to have differing opinions on the team.

If a founder is a risk-taker, they eventually need a voice in the room who is pragmatic, logical, and methodical—that is, risk averse. When the company is small, that risk-averse person can be viewed as a naysayer and no one wants that argument while they're still dreaming about validating the company.

Those pragmatic voices are important in a growing company, so discussions go deeper, and blind spots become visible. That voice will protect the company from a lot of mistakes. A founder may not be much of a "numbers person" (I hear this one a lot), but they will eventually need a numbers person who can challenge decisions on the basis of financial merit.

Founders become great CEOs when they can retire as General Manager of the Universe and bring on people who can carry out certain work, activities, and actions *better* than the founder. Some founders cannot separate themselves from this work, and that seldom ends well.

The Difference Between Team and Vendor Relationships

In my stint with one start-up, I was an employee; I owned the training and new employee orientation functions. Since I brought creativity and new thinking to this role, I was told by one of the board members (who was way too hands-on for someone without a title) "Kris, you're providing a service here, do you know what that means?" I was a little insulted, and it wasn't only because that statement is inherently condescending and in no way resembles a good leader attempting to tap into my best motivation. I was insulted because that's an abjectly poor way to build relationships interdepartmentally. My response was "I understand what it means to provide a service. Do you understand what a team is? Because we're a team, and that means we work together. Please don't treat me like a vendor."

My stance is that any organization should be aware that relationships within a company (usually interdepartmentally) are not unlike a marriage. They are a partnership, not an owner-vendor relationship. An organization has paid-service relationships with outside vendors and therefore has the right to hold all the authority in those relationships. Wielding authority in-house with colleagues and peers doesn't usually end well. Just like a marriage, one-way authority isn't sustainable. Even when someone's "in charge," they're not totally in charge. A balance must be struck, or the relationship just won't work.

I've gone so far as to recommend to clients in large organizations that one department cease treating another like a vendor, using those words. Internal "service providers" are usually experts and should be doing as much rule-setting around boundaries and expectations as the department receiving the service. I see this play out correctly in most IT functions. When a person stomps their feet and treats an IT team poorly in the name of getting what they want, their work life doesn't usually improve, and they may find their needs become a low priority. IT is normally seen as a team of experts, and they provide the rules and boundaries for people. The relationship is imperfect, but it's accepted.

What's important about being easy to follow is to understand that a great leader doesn't exist at the end of some mysterious journey full of books, conferences, classes, articles, degrees, etc. The great leader is in you now—today. Values that are visible to your team guide your behavior far more than a script or skill you're taught.

For all leaders, our values hold us accountable; they are our reassurance when we waver, and they set us back on our path when situations get difficult. Understanding and practicing mindfulness will translate into the practice of adhering to values—effortlessly. This is being easy to follow. This is being the best version of yourself as a leader.

CHAPTER 7

Being a Leader of Influence

I've already touched on the idea of taking advice with a grain of salt, to make sure it fits your circumstances, and to take away what works for you. Advice for how to handle an issue won't work in every circumstance; sometimes a leader also has to be able to switch styles, or wear a different hat for a while, to deal with something new or uncommon. This flexibility is a level of openness that makes any leader easier to follow.

Paradoxes of Being a Leader

Much has been written in recent years about *transformational* leadership. A common definition describes it in terms of leadership through growth and support of the individuals who follow the leader. It's very team focused and overcomes some of the tail chasing from putting the leader through constant leadership development training.

The goal is some level of valuable change in the followers. Transformational leadership can connect the follower's sense of self to a mission and the collective identity of the organization. At the center of transformational leadership is a leader acting as a role model for followers, to inspire and challenge them to take greater ownership of their work and results.

Transformational leadership is closely aligned with the values-based methods described in this book—to be easy to follow. A leader who becomes transformational, as it's described here, can be easier to follow in some ways.

Don't forget to look at everything with a critical eye and an open mind—and take away what you want to use. Transformational leadership is a great methodology with wide application. It is, however, just as imperfect as any other approach in its inability to universally fit all situations and all people. Many organizations have built transformational leadership as a cornerstone of behavior in their organization, without considering the possibility that it won't be the right approach for every circumstance.

There is a risk to that.

Here's where it can be dangerous. Transformational leadership has an antithesis: the authoritarian leadership style. Authoritarian leadership could loosely be described as one leader having full control over a group with minimal autonomy allowed within the ranks of the team and minimal input from the team. An authoritarian leader dictates policies, processes, behaviors, and the like, to be followed by their team without question.

Generally, twenty-first century workplaces in Western culture have an aversion to authoritarian leadership. Teams don't like it and leaders don't usually go there on purpose. The leaders who do rarely find sustained success in that role. People on teams just don't put up with it. For the sake of comparison, we'll call this style of authoritarian leadership "transactional."

Balance in Leadership

Seeing transformational leadership and transactional leadership as a dichotomy can help you understand that they should be part of the *same* leader. Imagine a lever that could toggle back and forth between these styles. I've learned that in almost every environment, there is a time and a place for a leader to be one style or the other.

Imagine a transformational leadership style in the emergency room of a hospital. Important events in that environment usually mean life-and-death situations. There's no time for a committee to get together and consider everyone's input. A leader has to step in and direct, and people have to follow. Decisions must be made in a split second. When an emergency has passed, there may be time to have mechanisms of transformational leadership to support individuals and team dynamics.

Transformational Versus Transactional

A well-rounded leader should be able to tap into both leadership styles to achieve what needs to be done. Living in only one camp is quite rigid and misses the opportunity to be versatile and adaptable. Sometimes, a leader must step in and move quickly without shocking the team. This means a leadership environment that is strictly transformational just doesn't lend itself to the occasional need to be transactional. The ideal leader is driven by values and can assume either role without looking manic or hypocritical to others. That is to say, what drives them to switch to and from transactional and transformational is clear to others.

When values drive your actions, you can use this lever to step into appropriate styles at the appropriate times. People see and understand your need to act appropriately.

The leader who is only transformational is just as limited and flawed as the transactional/authoritarian one, even if the former is more culturally acceptable in today's day and age.

Leadership levers like these exist in a few other dichotomies.

Control Versus Chaos

Tightly controlled environments can stifle innovation and creativity but can also limit the variations associated with waste. Some environments should be more controlled than others; think of a hospital operating room versus a tech start-up. At some point, the tech start-up may need to control some processes to save money or time. And an operating room should also have some built-in flexibility to adapt to complications or a sudden change in the care needed. Leaders are best equipped when they can maintain their values to use this lever to allow chaos when it's appropriate and exert control when it's appropriate as well. Environments can sometimes dictate this need.

The Ultimate Paradox: Two Things Motivate All People

When considering the various paradoxes of leadership—the things that live in a dichotomy yet are both needed situationally—

one stands out as the one leaders use the most. Leaders live in this dichotomy each and every day, whether they know it or not.

It's *motivation*.

Motivation. Managers seek it in themselves and their teams based on a simple premise: a human who is motivated will put in more effort for longer periods than someone who isn't. Putting in more effort *can* lead to higher productivity, more output, better collaboration, stronger work environment and teamwork, higher retention, and other possible benefits.

Simple enough, right? Yet even strong managers still fall into common traps, about what motivates people, that can alienate and isolate members of their team. Here are a just a few:

1. This is what motivates me, so others must like it too. This is a very observable trait in lazy leaders.

For example, if a leader has preferred private over public recognition their whole career, that leader may bestow private recognition onto others without asking them what they prefer. They don't consider that some people want public recognition, or that those people may feel underappreciated if they never get it. Leaders who practice only one of these types of recognition aren't likely to be giving *all* the individuals on their teams what they need—just the ones who like the same kind of recognition.

How do you know who likes public versus private recognition for their efforts? Maybe you have had a leader who assumed which you preferred, and they may have been incorrect. Are you doing the same to others? Have you ever just *asked* people to find out?

2. We have a motivational meeting or event every X (where X is some intermittent frequency such as quarterly or annually). Some leaders may think this is enough to motivate people, or nothing will. Leaders of all experience levels can default to "lazy" concerning this.

A personally beloved icon of the business world, the late Zig Ziglar, said, "Motivation doesn't last . . . neither does bathing. That's why I recommend it daily." If you just think about your day-to-day workflow, it's probably a little stressful, uncertain, or maybe even volatile. Things can change on a dime from success to setback to total catastrophe. Motivation is an all-the-time thing and must be maintained with the same diligence as hygiene. It has to be part of the culture.

What's your approach for motivating your team? What would be the harm in finding ways to do it that are more creative and more frequent? Have you asked your best teammates what they need to be motivated? Don't assume you know, if you've never asked.

3. When it comes to motivation or management, I am very black and white; I treat everyone the same, that way no one can say I am unfair. Sound familiar? This is the laziest leader of them all; often stemming from realizing it's hard to balance equitability and fairness, they use simple black-and-white rules (i.e., the path of least resistance).

Equitability and fairness are different, as previously discussed. Leaders truly earn their pay navigating the messy, uncertain, ambiguous gray areas in between the black and white.

If you are entrenched in being a black-and-white or one-size-fits-all leader, consider this: engineers write algorithms to navigate black-and-white scenarios. It's the simplest landscape for programming. Similarly, chimpanzees have been trained to learn and function in a similar setting of black/white or cause/effect. That means if you are a black-and-white kind of leader, you could be replaced with a simple machine or a chimp. I'll say it again: leaders earn their keep by operating successfully in the areas of grey. And most areas have shades of grey.

4. Motivation is complicated. No, it's actually simple, but you can't tell from what's being written about it. A search on Amazon late in 2017 yielded over 214,000 titles of books written on the topic of motivation. Two years earlier, that number was 86,000. This deep pool of titles illustrates a) the high importance of this topic and b) the labyrinth of complexity people find when navigating it. Compare it to, say, a similar search on "building a wooden chair," which yields around 30 titles. There must be countless possibilities for making a chair, but the best practices are simple and easy to demonstrate; i.e., there may be little disagreement about what works best. Motivation, on the other hand, can be far more subjective.

Getting too academic can be ineffective. If you think you need to sit with your team and discuss Maslow's hierarchy of needs, intrinsic versus extrinsic motivators, and *Theory X* versus *Theory Y* of motivation, you'll see people go cross-eyed trying to act interested. Some may love it, but for others it's downright boring. And there's no need—because all that complexity boils down to two things.

Only Two Things Motivate All People

Consider this concept the most important one you can take from this work: *only two things* motivate people. Can you name one?

When asked, the most common answer that comes up is *money*. Then comes *recognition*, followed by things that may be related to those like *benefits*, *kudos*, etc.

They are wrong. Not totally off base, but wrong nonetheless. What are the two things that motivate all people to action?

Fear and desire are the two things that motivate all people.

Everything you can think of will fall into one of those two categories.

Money? Money is not a motivator by itself. The *desire* to have a lot (or the *things* it can buy) can be. Likewise, the *fear* of not having enough money and the consequences related to it can also be a motivator. Those are two totally different situations. Someone in one of those situations is likely to be in a completely separate mental state than someone in the other; how they act and perform is different, too. Most importantly, how they respond to their leader's actions will also be different.

I hear many sales managers proudly proclaim they only want people motivated by money. But what is such a person actually motivated by? What value is important to them? Sales managers are much better served by seeking more specific values in their sales people: people who are competitive, courageous, enthusiastic. Simply asking for people who are money motivated can invite in people with varying levels of integrity and ethics, and such a motivation may be unrelated to what will actually get them up in the morning: their fears and/or desires.

Success? Again, not a motivator. That word alone doesn't help me motivate someone to be successful. Success may bring desire to be competitive and beat others, or it may have little to do with winning and more to do with wanting to be the center of attention.

Both are constructs of success, but you may motivate a competitor much differently than you would a prima donna type.

Without even knowing it consciously, every leader uses *fear* and *desire* daily (that includes *you*). The fear-based manager has a tone of "or else," and it's implicit in most of their leadership. They may say things like, "Just be happy you have a job," "Everyone's replaceable," or "You *need* to (blank; some difficult or challenging activity)." They can be very one size fits all when it comes to how they treat others as a way to not make mistakes.

Leaders sometimes build a fear-based culture innocently; they are not *trying* to make people afraid. Most are just trying to be tough, strong, or the like. As previously stated, "If tough love is done properly, it should only be *tough* on the person giving it. If done right, it's far easier on the receiver." The fear-based leader uses words like *mandatory* as a crutch to get actions they think are important.

I can tell you from firsthand experience, nothing takes the fun out of things like calling them mandatory. Watch, I'll prove it: after your morning coffee tomorrow, you will have mandatory cupcakes. See? Even cupcakes sound awful when you make them mandatory (if you disagree, it's okay to admit part of you was immediately resistant or skeptical of a "mandatory cupcake").

Want to improve as a leader? Remove the word mandatory from your regular vocabulary and hold yourself accountable to connect people and the importance of a particular action to a value. Think about *what's in it for them.* Rather than people acting in a way because they have to, they are doing it because they know it's important, even if unpleasant.

Think about it. The best leaders you've seen could just level with you, and you respected that even if what they said was difficult and stung when you heard it. Believe me, it's much harder to package that message in a way that earned your respect and *motivated* you (see what I did there . . . ?) to improve.

The desire-based leader works every day to tap into *why* each individual is there and what they like or need at work. Instead of saying things like, "You're lucky to have a job," they say "We're (I'm) lucky to have you here." They put regular intention into understanding what their people need to feel valued and important, and how to help them get there and stay there when they may stray.

It should be explicit here that a leader who tries to motivate by tapping into people's desires will have stronger trust, more valuable communication, and likely better long-term results than the leader who motivates by preying on people's fears. Moreover, values expressed by such a leader are likely to align with the needs of their teams and the work to be done.

The fear-based culture runs the risk of having individuals who are isolated and do just enough to get by, rarely innovating or trying to risk anything with extra effort. Fear-based motivation simply isn't sustainable. It wears on people and accelerates burnout. And who resigns first? It's never who you hoped, is it? Your top performers and most talented stars get fed up first and are the first ones to realize they want (and can find) greener pastures.

What Does a Fear-Based or a Desire-Based Culture Look Like?

What kind of culture do *you* create? A culture of fear? A culture of desire? These are some symptoms of a fear-based culture versus a desire-based culture *(warning: self-awareness coming)*:

Fear: People just show up.	**Desire**: People are *present.*
Fear: People do just enough to get by, and watch the clock.	**Desire**: People go above and beyond regularly and enjoy doing it.
Fear: People shut up and do their job.	**Desire**: People are involved, vocal, and engaged.
Fear: People need more direction and correction.	**Desire**: People tend to find their own way, or the best way.
Fear: People view many things as big, critical problems—they are problem-finders.	**Desire**: People are problem-solvers—they try things on their own to get better.
Fear: People can't wait to leave.	**Desire**: People can't wait to get there.
Fear: People hear "This is mandatory."	**Desire**: People hear "This is valuable."

Get the picture? If you see more of the fear behavior in your environment, then you need to look at your style with a critical eye. If you are the kind of person who makes things *mandatory*, it means you are poor at tapping into the desires of others to be successful.

Instead of saying, "This training is mandatory, so complete it," try "This training is an important part of our team being (*insert appropriate value*). It may be inconvenient, but I want you to go." You've now connected it to something important: a value.

So how do you become better at creating a culture where people are motivated by desire (team pride, achievement, recognition, or some other values) rather than fear (things to avoid: a bad evaluation, warnings, alienation)? Here's a short case study:

> Organization X underwent a pay-raise freeze for one year. During that year, staff attendance for department meetings dropped from 80 percent to around 40 percent. Managers responded by making all meetings mandatory, and the blowback was people felt pushed around; it was punitive on top of not getting a raise. Here's what happened: most departments (not the whole company) had a policy in place that if you didn't attend at least 80 percent of the meetings in a year, you were not eligible for the maximum annual pay raise and you'd be capped at the minimum annual pay raise. This policy persisted for years until the year of the freeze on all raises. People responded to the freeze by not coming to meetings. They were no longer afraid of losing money by missing meetings.

The motivation to attend the meetings was based on avoiding a negative consequence: that's fear based. Make no mistake, there was no desire there; people were behaving to avoid a negative consequence.

This case study was a prime example of how leaders can very innocently rule by fear. Thinking it was a money motivator, it ended up being an "or else." The stronger leaders at this company had high meeting attendance that continued through the year of the pay freeze because they made meetings about the team; meetings were fun, people left them with a stronger love and/or respect for their job and their teammates. People had desire to attend the meetings even when it was inconvenient to do so.

The leaders with struggling attendance during the pay freeze usually made their meetings just about the critical information and were scared to spend any more time with fun or interesting things. They thought it was a headache just getting staff to come in the first place, so why add anything "fluffy"?

Caution: Leaders can lead with values, and still be building a fear-driven workplace.

To see the most robust example of how fear and desire motivate us, one need not look further than the 2016/2017 landscape of politics and news. If you remember the extensive coverage of the 2016 presidential primary campaign and the ensuing presidency, the tactics used were fear-based. When a leader or news organization uses fear as a motivator, it's actually easier to get a reaction, i.e., someone is more likely to act to avoid or prevent danger than to receive some sort of benefit. Consider these common scenarios that play out all around us:

- Many people may be more likely to change their diet after a heart attack than to prevent one.
- Many people say they "perform better" when under pressure rather than working ahead.
- Many people can swim, but if you saw a shark behind you, I promise you'll find that "little extra" to speed up.

Get it? If someone wants to create urgency, they can either tell you . . . "If we don't hit our deadline, they'll have our heads!" . . . Or, they can tell you . . . "If we hit our deadline, they're going to love us!"

While the former will get more people to see the importance, the latter is actually better for long-term motivations. The problem with fear-based motivation is that over time, people simply burn out on it and quit, or become desensitized to it.

So now to the landscape of politics and news coverage. Listen closely to the biggest moments of the news cycles. Most politicians, especially when running for office, lean heavily on fear-based motivation. Even though it may be a little ungenuine, it's a good strategy: they only have a short window to motivate voters to act (where acting is to rally, volunteer, donate, and/or vote).

When I listened to candidates on the campaign, nearly every statement was preying on fear. The desire-based motivation would be a candidate inspiring people about the vision and work they themselves can do; their values would be openly on display. However, most candidates find it easier to create fear connected to the consequences of supporting their opponent. The most obvious is when candidates discuss terrorism. It's very easy to make people afraid for their lives; but notice how all of a sudden, the threat of terror is at its peak every four years? If you dig a little in the headlines, equally scary things were happening 30 and 40 years ago. In a more general sense, the Middle East has had unrest for many centuries, and therefore the threat of terror worldwide has been around just as long.

Candidates know they can create more action by instilling fear than by creating desire. The problem is, they have to position themselves on the opposite end of that fear. They will seldom phrase their stump speech as, *"If you vote for me, you'll get (positive outcome)."*

You're much more likely to hear the statement as, *"If you **don't** vote for me, then (negative outcome) will happen."*

And if candidates can associate those fears with their competitors, it's even **more** likely that you'll hear, *"If you vote for (opponent), you'll get (negative consequence)."*

It's rare for people to refer to any of the campaigns as a "movement." It takes a very diverse group (by age, race, income, gender, etc.) with fierce loyalty to call it a movement. It's fascinating to see that much passion; good leaders know that passion and enthusiasm can be contagious. Whether it's a political campaign or a workplace, at the center of such a movement is a deep connection to desire-based motivation. What ignites that motivation? Values.

If a leader uses fear (even if not on purpose) to drive a team, they risk wrapping their arms around a fickle concept. Consider our presidential primaries, where a candidate spends their campaign cutting down their opponent, but later endorses them as the nominee. Few things seem more ungenuine—even hypocritical.

If a candidate spent their campaign focused on their own vision, connecting that vision to the nominee wouldn't be anywhere near as hypocritical. The other challenge with fear is that it can wane easily. Leaders who lean on fear-based motivation (with mandatories, or-else threats, and other consequence-based rules) find that people adapt quickly to avoid consequences, doing just enough to avoid the consequence, not necessarily excelling or succeeding. Leaders find themselves jumping quickly to the next bigger or scarier fear. If you've ever wondered why some cultures treat new rules or initiatives like a "flavor of the month," you now know what's at play. That is a fear-based culture with leaders who unintentionally peddle that fear. When people are surrounded by the negative consequences in a workplace, it makes them do just enough to not fail. Does that sound like engagement to you?

I ask all leaders and mangers to take a lesson from the landscape of politics and news cycles; fear is a powerful motivator, but it's far less substantive than desire.

Fear can get people to move, but desire will make them fiercely loyal. Loyal colleagues will demonstrate passion and perseverance.

A leader who uses desire as her or his main tool will be seen as visionary, passionate, and as someone with high integrity. Some will view that leader as an unrealistic dreamer, but let's keep perspective. When values are open, expressed, and aligned, you are set up for desire-based motivation in that environment.

Now consider the value of the paradox. In a desire-based workplace, a leader may occasionally need to build in a dire situation or dire consequence in order to create situational urgency, like a contract you are about to lose, or a sudden deadline, or service recovery. Fear may creep in and it may get heightened effort and results. It is also not sustainable. Like every paradox, a leader must understand both of these, and at all times understand which they are using to build influence or wield authority.

Conclusion

People connect with and follow values. Take the time to know what your values are and make them clear to others. Getting to know yourself so you know what your values are will make you a better leader. If you haven't started that introspective process yet, make that commitment. Then share who you are with your team. Let *them* get to know you better: when you communicate your values, demonstrate them, and recognize the ones you want your team to display, they understand you more as a leader. You will create genuine common ground and connections with them.

Work has more meaning for everyone involved when you know why things are done the way they are. Communication, motivation, change management, transparency, performance improvement, and teamwork all feel different and more honest when you are easy to follow.

Your values are inherently simple and easy to understand. When they are clearly expressed, a leader's hang-ups, skill gaps, or other shortcomings are reduced or minimized. They become irrelevant, and teams want to follow the person, not the skill.

Leadership Development Isn't a Journey; Being a Leader Is the Journey

Early in my career, I learned one of my greatest lessons from a leader I admired—a manager who had such enthusiasm for his work, you could see it in his teams and colleagues; it was infectious. His primary role was to develop the company's new leaders.

This leader once recounted a conversation with one of his direct reports, someone who ran a local branch office within his division. This young manager was struggling with holding others accountable and driving strong results. He was seeing mediocrity when the aim was excellence.

This leader responded with something I wasn't expecting and haven't heard since. He looked that manager in the eye and said: "Quit being so selfish."

At first, I couldn't make a connection from a leader's selfishness and an office's mediocre results. He went on to say, "You're being selfish . . . you're imposing your own shortcomings on your team. You're young and inexperienced, and because of this you're tentative . . . timid. You're holding yourself back, so your team isn't getting the best 'you.' Only the best 'you' can bring out the best 'them.' Your people aren't succeeding because of your own hang-ups and fears."

This was heavy. It would probably be inappropriate in most contexts. There's something deep and profound about it too, and I wanted to share this same statement with you without hurting your feelings, in case it applies to you: everyone has hang-ups and fears. Yours are holding you back.

I don't know you, but I *am* talking about you, make no mistake about it. Whatever level of success you have achieved or are achieving—if you are a leader, every ounce of your unused ability translates to a limitation on the people who depend on you. What does that really mean? It means there's always something you can improve.

Humans are like any other living organism. Always be growing. Consider plants: they are either growing or dying. There is no status quo.

When I work with nursing groups, one of the topics we discuss is stress and its effect on teamwork. When we're tired, anxious, or stressed in any way, we're not at our best. That's when little things like eye rolls or under-communication can happen. I state clearly to these groups that if teamwork isn't working well, it's impossible for patient care to be optimal. If an individual isn't at their best (i.e., stressed), teamwork can't be either.

Talented nurses can still provide great care, but teams are kidding themselves if they think what they are doing is optimal patient care while the team is exhausted and stressed. It says a lot about nurses that they can be very successful and provide a high level of care despite this. Pointing out the impact of stress on teamwork and the patient care always gets their attention, and I have repeatedly seen how nursing groups achieve more of their potential when they treat their teammates with the same care and tolerance their patients receive—when organizations and leaders recognize how important it is to take care of the people who take care of patients. The same attitude applies beyond nursing teams to any organization.

The Easy to Follow Leader

While your workplace may not have life and death at stake, you have important work to do. I can say with every bit of confidence that, as a leader, your hang-ups interfere with the success of those who depend on you. When you aren't transparent, when you miss an opportunity to show courage, when you are not present, when you stray from a value and don't address it, you are not easy to follow. By contrast, when you are trying too hard to flip the needle in the opposite direction, you could lose relatability and authenticity.

A leader can do a lot of things to make or break the relationships around them. When there is a coherent set of values, relationships have a foundation. Leaders set the tone, but clear values echo and affect everyone, whether or not the leader is in the room. It's how people self-govern effectively. The benefits are boundless. It's simple; and it's the most authentic way to lead. It's an extension of you.

Be easy to follow.

Appendix

List of Core Values

Choose 6-8 values from this list with the goal of narrowing it down to 6 or fewer. See organizational values exercise in chapter 4. Ask yourself: Why is this value important to me?

Acceptance/Tolerance	Authenticity	Challenge
Accomplishment	Authority	Charity
Accountability	Autonomy	Citizenship
Accuracy	Balance	Cleanliness
Achievement	Beauty	Clarity
Adaptability/Flexibility	Boldness	Comfort
Adventure	Bravery/Courage	Commitment
Altruism	Brilliance/Intelligence	Common Sense
Ambition	Care	Communication (what
Amusement	Calm	kind)
Assertiveness	Candor	Community
Attentive	Capability	Compassion
Attention to Detail	Carefulness	Competence
Awareness	Certainty	Concentration

Confidence	Enjoyment	Happiness
Conflict	Enthusiasm	Hard Work
Contribution	Equality	Harmony
Connection	Ethics	Health
Consciousness	Etiquette	Honesty
Consistency	Excellence	Honor
Contentment	Experience	Hope
Contribution	Expertise	Humility
Control	Giving/Generosity	Humor
Conviction	Exploration/Curiosity	Imagination
Cooperation	Expressiveness/	Improvement
Courage/Bravery	Openness	Independence
Courtesy	Fairness	Individuality
Creativity	Family	Influence
Credibility	Fame	Inner Harmony
Curiosity	Fearlessness	Innovation
Decisiveness	Feelings/Sympathy	Insightfulness
Dedication	Ferociousness	Inspiration
Dependability	Fierceness	Integrity
Determination	Fidelity	Intelligence
Development	Focus	Intensity
Devotion	Foresight	Intuition
Dignity	Fortitude	Irreverence
Discipline	Following the Rules	Joy
Discovery	Freedom	Justice
Drive	Friendship	Kindness
Disagreement	Fun	Knowledge
Effectiveness	Generosity	Lawfulness
Efficiency	Genius	Learning
Empathy	Goodness	Liberty
Empowerment/	Going by the Book	Logic
Ambition/	Grace	Love
Independence	Gratitude	Loyalty
Endurance	Greatness	Mastery of Expertise
Energy (positive)	Growth	Maturity

Appendix

Meaningful Work
Moderation
Motivation
Openness
Optimism
Order
Organization
Originality
Partnership
Passion
Patience
Peace
Performance
Persistence
Playfulness
Poise
Politeness
Popularity
Potential
Power
Presence
Productivity
Professionalism
Prosperity
Purpose
Quality
Realism
Reasoning/Logic
Recognition
Recreation
Reflection/
   Introspection
Reliability
Religion
Reputation

Respect
Responsibility
Restraint
Results Oriented
Reverence
Rigor
Risk Tolerance
Risk Aversion
Satisfaction
Security
Self-Reliance
Self-Respect
Selfless
Sensitivity
Serenity
Service
Sharing
Significance
Silence
Simplicity
Sincerity
Skillfulness
Solitude
Spirituality
Spontaneous
Stability
Status
Stewardship
Strength
Structure
Success
Support
Surprise
Sustainability
Talent

Teamwork
Temperance
Thankfulness
Thoroughness
Thoughtfulness
Timeliness
Tolerance
Toughness
Tradition
Tranquility
Transparency
Trust/Trustworthiness
Truth/Honesty
Understanding
Uniqueness
Unity
Valor
Vigor
Vision
Vitality
Wealth
Welcoming
Winning
Wisdom
Wonder
Zeal

What Are Your Values?

1.

    _____

2.

    _____

3.

    _____

4.

    _____

5.

_____

6.

_____

7.

_____

8.

_____

Today you are You,
that is truer than true.
There is no one alive
who is Youer than You.

—Dr. Seuss

Acknowledgments

It's important to me that those who are most responsible for my success and my path are mentioned thoughtfully here.

John Kane—the first person to teach me the importance of listening to your heart, truly caring for those around you, and following your values.

Rick Castro—where I learned tough love meant being tough on yourself and tough on your own limitations.

Vector Marketing—from age 18-26, there was no better place for me, as a young leader, to learn from what is still the best group of leaders I've ever met.

Morgan Smith—she took a chance on me in the most improbable of circumstances, then believed in me like no one else has, then gave me the support I needed to thrive. Everything I achieve comes from how she took me from acorn to oak.

The Catholic Medical Center family—for the footprints on my heart.

David Band—who taught me the totally unique dimension of working with C-suite executive teams. His work and advice have been enormously successful for me.

Farrah Deselle—teachers emerge from the most unexpected places. Thank you for challenging my view of the world.

Catherine Belanger—who taught me to lean into my conscience with confidence. Without her, there is no Bushido Leadership.

A special thanks to the team at Aloha Publishing, whose diligent work and guidance brought this work to life.

Mom—few people on earth are as capable of giving so fully of themselves as she is. She is the gold standard for my generosity of heart. And I try every day to live up to that.

About the Author

Kris Mailepors is an award-winning talent professional with degrees in business and the sciences. An executive coach, positive change consultant, and speaker, Kris works to throw a lifeline to leaders who are overwhelmed by their environment of unrealistic workloads, constant change, hazy expectations, and volatile uncertainty. He takes successful disciplines and shares simple and practical ways to live them in the twenty-first century landscape. For over 20 years, Kris has shaped leaders in healthcare, finance, retail, automotive, and other industries with his completely unique and fresh approaches to thriving as a leader. A simple motto drives his work: ***better leaders create better results.***

This work centers around the concept that professional growth is a deeply personal undertaking and can never be one size fits all. That one-size-fits-all approach has failed the tens of thousands of smart, talented leaders who flunk their first year of management. Kris believes strongly that the best version of yourself doesn't exist at the end of some mysterious journey of attending classes and conferences; it already exists in you this very moment. With what you have right now, you can live the best you; you can be your best leader.

Kris is passionate about experiencing nature through exploring, hiking, biking, and camping. In his spare time, he supports youth services including the Boys and Girls Club. He takes his dog, SunnyBear, with him whenever he can.

Kris completed his MBA at the University of Otago in New Zealand, where some of the world's best business minds engage with students.

For more of Bushido's writings, or to inquire about leadership development that will forever change you and your leaders, visit BushidoLeadership.com. To book SunnyBear for a guest appearance or for any other question, email kris@bushidoleadership.com.

Acknowledgments

SunnyBear

AS A LEADER, HAVE YOU EVER ASKED YOURSELF, "AM I EASY TO FOLLOW?"

No other leader can tell you what kind of leader to be. That's a personal set of values that will eliminate the workplace culture problems most teams experience and get them to peak performance.

The best leader you'll ever be doesn't exist at the end of some mysterious journey to be reached later in your career. That leader already exists in you this very moment.

If this book resonates with you, please post a review on Amazon, spread the word in social media, pass on what you have learned to your colleagues, and reach out to me at Kris@bushidoleadership. com. I'd love to hear about your leadership journey and how I can help you.

Connect with Kris Mailepors on LinkedIn
Like @bushidoleadership on Facebook
Follow @bushidoleader on Twitter
Follow Bushido Leadership on Google+
Email Kris@bushidoleadership.com

EasytoFollowLeader.com